Tut,
Hope you enjoy!
Rod Cate

GET BACK UP

A MEMOIR ON HOW TO NOT ALLOW A DEVASTATING LIFE-
CHANGING EVENT RUIN YOUR QUEST FOR A GREAT LIFE.

BY: ROD CATE

D1506511

There is nothing better than trying cases. Even though I knew this case was going to end badly, I enjoyed trying it right up until the time the jury returned its verdict. Preparation for a trial like *Luna* is excruciatingly hard and exhausting. Developing trial strategies, working with witnesses and preparing for the trial demanded several weeks of preparation. By the time the trial actually started, I had worked 30 days in a row. It is typical, though, for any lawyer trying a case to be exhausted when the case begins.

Even though the trial ended in a loss, I was actually pleased with my performance. One of the most frustrating parts about being a trial lawyer is that no matter how well you perform at trial, you can still lose. You can't change the facts, and more importantly, you don't usually get to select the cases you want to try, especially as a defense lawyer. In contrast, the lawyers who represented Luna carefully screen all potential cases and typically only choose to take on cases where their chances of winning are extremely high and the potential damages are astronomical.

I was receiving compliments during the trial by several of the spectators and other lawyers. The paralegal for Memorial Hospital stopped me in the hallway and told me she loved watching me in front of the jury. My head naturally inflated. However, it was short-lived because no matter how well you think you're doing, or how well you actually are doing, it doesn't matter. The only thing that does matter is the verdict, which is for a group of twelve strangers to decide. Nothing compares with the thrill of being in front of a jury, especially winning. On the other hand, losing a trial is about the most devastating thing I've experienced.

Although the jury awarded the enormous verdict, I actually settled the case for InTran minutes before the jury reached its monumental verdict. The settlement amount is confidential, but I can say InTran's CEO and CFO were extremely pleased with the result. Walking out of the courthouse with my clients, my ego was crushed. But, most importantly, my clients were ecstatic over the settlement. Later that evening, a reporter called me and asked for a comment on the verdict. I put my best spin on the verdict as I knew my quote would end up in the local paper: "Fortunately, we settled the case before the jury returned its verdict. Although the verdict amount is disappointing, it was inconsequential to my client." Of course, I didn't comment on how personally crushing the verdict was.

In my 25-year career, I've tried several big cases, and I've done fairly well with them. I've always felt I have a good rapport with juries, which is one reason the *Luna* verdict was so devastating. Apparently, the jury bought nothing I was trying to sell.

CHAPTER TWO
MY INJURY

The second reason it was difficult for me to walk out of the Baldwin County Courthouse after the *Luna* verdict was that I am an ambulatory quadriplegic. This means I have some paralysis in every part of my body from the neck down, but can walk. I am probably one of the few quadriplegics in the world who can actually walk. I was 15 years old in 1981 when I broke my neck playing high school football. I was about to enter South Stokes High School in Walnut Cove, North Carolina as one of the most heralded athletes in the school's history. I recognize "heralded" is an incredibly pretentious word to describe yourself, but let's just say I was pretty damn good. I played and excelled in all sports. I played quarterback and free safety and led our team to an undefeated season in the ninth grade. In one game, I threw for over 400 yards and five touchdowns. I averaged 20 points a game in basketball. I played baseball and ran track. My high school athletic career was going to be stellar - the only question was where I was going to play college football.

My high school athletic career ended before it even began. We had just finished a grueling week of preseason camp prior to the beginning of school. We lived at the high school and went through "three-a-days" practicing in full pads at dawn and late afternoon and in shorts and helmets right after lunch to work on special teams. Camp went extremely well. I won the starting free safety job on the varsity team and was also making a push to be the starting quarterback. Only two rising sophomores made the varsity.

Camp culminated with an intra-squad scrimmage under lights on Friday night. The game was open to the public and there was a sizeable crowd. This was my first opportunity to play in front of a big crowd. I couldn't wait – probably a little too jacked up. The scrimmage started with the first team defense taking on a thrown-together offense. Back in those days, the best players played both ways, so many of the starters on defense were also starters on the offense. My brother Mike, a junior and starting cornerback, was to

My neurosurgeon was a great guy, Dr. Mike McWhorter, who I recently learned died several years ago. He was a big ole guy who played football at Mississippi State. Dr. McWhorter was the chief neurosurgeon at Baptist Hospital where he taught neurosurgeon residents at Wake Forest. He had bright red hair and a very gregarious personality. He laughed and smiled a lot. I took an instant liking to him. The surgery was a success in that my neck was stabilized. Dr. McWhorter explained that had my spinal cord been severed, I would never move again. Because the spinal cord was just badly bruised, there was a chance (emphasis on "chance") I would regain some movement and feeling. However, Dr. McWhorter made it clear there was a good chance I would never walk again.

Maybe because of my youth or maybe because my brain would not allow me to comprehend the gravity of my situation, I didn't react one way or the other to the explanation of my condition. I was always upbeat in the days following the surgery. I smiled and laughed with my family and friends who came to visit me. My smile was actually genuine. Oddly, I was never depressed. My life had been forever changed, but for some reason, I was always genuinely upbeat. Maybe my condition hadn't set in yet. After a couple of weeks, my physicians thought my emotional response was abnormal since I was never down. I underwent several psychological tests and counseling sessions, but no one found anything abnormal.

I remained in Baptist Hospital for a month following the surgery. Days were spent lying in bed. I was turned from side to side every few hours to prevent bed sores. I remember all the fruit baskets and flowers filling my room. I received photographs from Bear Bryant and Johnny Majors with notes attached, as well as cards and well wishes from other college coaches. My Mom was with me every day. The days were long and excruciatingly boring. I was taking a heavy dose of steroids prescribed to help reduce the swelling in my bruised spinal cord. Dr. McWhorter explained that although my spinal cord had been permanently damaged, he hoped I might regain some movement and sensation as the swelling subsided.

I remained motionless and could feel nothing for more than three weeks after the surgery. To make matters worse, the steroids caused my face to break out with horrendous acne. I remember lying in my hospital bed paralyzed, bald, and covered in acne. The acne itched horribly, but I could not move my hands to rub my face to relieve it. The constant itching, the inability to feel anything or move, having to be fed, and lying in the bed constantly, finally got to me.

As if that wasn't enough, something else happened. One of the orderlies I had come to know was joking around with me when he came to empty my urinal (I was being catheterized and also using a urinal when I needed it). He thought I had a non-spill urinal that did not leak back out of the top. But it wasn't. He thought he was pretending to throw the pee in the urinal on me. It was not pretend. The pee went all over me. That same day was the first time I looked at myself in the mirror since my accident. I had always been a pretty good looking guy. What I saw in the mirror was just shocking – a bald head and a puffy face covered in acne from the steroids. I didn't even recognize myself. That day was just too much. Three weeks into the ordeal, I finally broke down and cried. I wept for about five minutes straight. I asked my mom, *"Why me?"* I think she actually felt some relief that I had finally broken down. She knew it was not normal for someone to keep all of these emotions inside. After the five minutes of weeping, I never cried again about my situation or asked, *"Why me?"*

The next day, I was looking down at my uncovered feet in the bed. I wanted to try to move my legs but had no idea how to go about it. I remember trying to remember what it felt like to point my toes down. I did it in my mind. When I looked down, I saw the toe on my left foot next to my pinky toe move. No one else was in the room to see what had just happened. I didn't know if this was a fluke or if my toe had actually moved. I tried again. The same toe moved. Looking back on it, I don't remember being that excited about purposefully moving a body part for the first time. But it was a big deal, and it was the beginning of the long road back.

As the swelling in my spinal cord began to further subside, I started to regain some movement in other parts of my body. Just as important, my feeling began to return. This process happened rapidly. I could move all my toes and legs within a week after first moving my toe. It was interesting that movement started first in my lower extremities. I began going through the beginnings of rehab in the hospital. I was placed on a rolling bed and taken to a rehab room at the end of the hall. The therapist moved me to a table and started to tilt me toward an upright position. Lying in the bed for so long without being able to stand up resulted in dizziness when my head was elevated toward a standing position. A successful day would be increasing the angle of the table in the rehab room to where I would not pass out or throw up. Eventually, I was able to withstand the steepest angle, almost 90 degrees to the floor, while not fainting or puking all over myself.

several of the partners took me out for a very nice dinner and after dinner drinks. I was a little hung over during the interviews the next day, but I was used to performing with a hangover. Looking back on it, it never entered my mind during my interviews that I was handicapped. I never considered what these people were thinking of me walking the way that I did. It must have been some kind of a shock to the lawyers who interviewed me when I showed up walking all messed up. None of these lawyers had any forewarning I was handicapped. For some reason, especially in my 20s, I never thought of myself as being handicapped or stopped to think how other people viewed me.

On my return flight to Chapel Hill from Mobile, I got stuck in Nashville, Tennessee because of snow and ice. By the time I arrived in Chapel Hill, after a two-day delay in Nashville, I had waiting for me in my mailbox a job offer for a summer clerkship position from Armbrecht Jackson. I accepted the position and spent part of the summer of 1989 in Mobile, Alabama.

Prior to my first summer clerkship position, I did not own a suit. Looking back on it, I must have interviewed in a blazer and slacks. I did not even appreciate the difference between a blazer and slacks and a suit. I referred to blazer and slacks as a suit. I guess growing up in small towns and seldom having to dress up, I never focused or took the time to understand the particulars of dress clothes. Before I traveled to Mobile for my summer clerkship, I went to a discount suit store and bought two wool suits. At the time, I did not know the difference between tropical weight, worsted, or any other kind of wool suit. The suits I bought were heavy wool. I bought some button-down collar shirts, some ties and dress shoes, and a matching belt, and off I went to the Deep South. I grew up in Tennessee, Virginia, and North Carolina where it was hot in the summertime, but it was nothing like that summer I experienced in Mobile. I showed up in Mobile in a red Chevy S-10 pickup with no air conditioning that my father had loaned me to take to law school.

Armbrecht Jackson was one of the two large "silk stocking" defense firms in Mobile, Alabama. Being a summer clerk in this type of highly respected firm was the greatest job I ever had. A summer clerkship position is a time for the law student to impress the law firm not only as to the law student's intelligence and legal abilities, but also how the law student would fit in with the firm's culture.

The amount of wining and dining was just incredible. On top of the wining and dining was the $700 per week salary, by far the most money I had ever made. At the end of my first clerkship I was invited back for the next summer and accepted the position. Because I felt comfortable with the Armbrecht Jackson firm and really liked being on the Gulf Coast, I accepted an associate position offer and began my career as a real lawyer following my graduation from North Carolina in 1992.

CHAPTER TEN
STARTING MY CAREER
AS A LAWYER

I arrived in Mobile, Alabama in late May 1992 to begin my legal career. I was still driving the red pickup truck with no air conditioning. I arrived with all my suitcases in the bed of the truck, moved into an apartment, and began an abbreviated summer of work before studying for the bar exam. My annual first year associate salary was $50,000, plus a $6,000 signing bonus. For someone who had never made more than minimum wage, this was a tremendous amount of money.

Being a first-year associate was a 180-degree change from being a second-year summer law clerk. The wining and dining was over. As a first-year associate, you were expected to do any legal job anyone at the firm asked you to do, to do it well, and to bill as many hours as you could. (And be fucking happy about it!) When I started working in the early nineties, the judicial system in Alabama was like the Wild Wild West. The Alabama Supreme Court was one of the most liberal state supreme courts in the country. Punitive damage awards of millions of dollars were the norm even in cases where actual damages were minimal. Juries award punitive damages to punish a defendant and deter similar conduct. Compensatory or actual damages, as the term indicates, are awarded to compensate a plaintiff for damages caused by a defendant's conduct. Alabama was known nationally as "tort hell." Mobile County was one of the most feared counties in Alabama as large jury verdicts were commonplace. I could not have picked a better place to begin my legal career. There was so much litigation work in my firm that billing 2,300 to 2,400 hours each year was easy. That's pretty good production.

I was fortunate that, early on, I began working with a partner who had a client with over 50 lawsuits filed against it throughout the State of Alabama. So instead of spending hour after hour in the library doing legal research, I quickly became a "real lawyer" taking depositions and attending hearings throughout the State. I became involved in class action cases and complex litigation by my second year. The great thing about class actions is the lawyers representing both sides are typically excellent lawyers from whom a second-year associate could learn much. Moreover, the stakes in class actions are extremely high, and the legal work is quite challenging.

On top of all that, travel is extensive. In the first major class action case I handled, I traveled throughout the United States, including Chicago, New York, Miami, Richmond, Memphis, Dallas, and Atlanta. Although I loved traveling because I really enjoyed seeing different cities, my physical limitations made traveling extremely difficult. The traveling I did in the early to mid-nineties was before rolling suitcases. Not only did I have to lug a suitcase to the check-in counter, I had to carry a heavy briefcase full of documents. I refused to ride in a wheelchair to the gate. My pride simply would not allow it. During that time, I became very familiar with several airports, especially Atlanta, and dreaded when I had a tight connection. I would jump on an electric cart - not as degrading as a wheelchair. The problem with electric carts is they were never there when I needed one.

The first time I flew to Atlanta when I was actually staying in Atlanta and not connecting, I got off of the underground train at the wrong stop. I mistakenly assumed the T Gates (ticketing) was also the stop for the front of the airport where I could get a taxi. I got off one stop early. By the time I lugged my suitcase a couple hundred yards with no end of the long hallway in sight, I realized I had made a mistake. About 300 yards later and soaking wet with sweat, I finally reached the escalator that took me to baggage claim and ground transportation. I like taking escalators as opposed to elevators – much more of a challenge timing the step on and off.

Things could not have been any better for a young defense lawyer than they were for me. Because of the multiple large verdicts in Alabama, companies and their insurance carriers were mortified anytime they were sued there and spared no expense in defending lawsuits - a defense lawyer's dream. Bills were never questioned. Cases were staffed with multiple lawyers. If I was not traveling throughout the country, I was traveling the highways of Alabama going from court to court. All of this was too good to last. And it didn't.

The plaintiffs' lawyers in Alabama killed the "golden goose." There seemed to be a competition among them to see who could get the largest punitive damages verdict. Ego and greed shut the circus down. For the greater benefit of society, this was probably a good thing. However, when your livelihood depends on being paid to defend lawsuits, the last thing you want to see is the potential for your client to get popped with a large verdict go away. Although you never want your client to get hit with a large verdict, having other companies get popped continued the fear and the "spare no expense defense strategy."

In the mid-nineties, the U.S. Supreme Court case of *BMW v. Gore* was the first shot across the bow for runaway verdicts, not only in Alabama but across the country. The BMW case originated in Alabama. The plaintiff, Dr. Ira Gore, purchased a new BMW from a dealer in Birmingham, Alabama. Dr. Gore wanted to make his BMW look "snazzier than it normally would appear" and took his BMW to a company called "Slick Finish" to "snazzy-up the BMW." Mr. Slick found evidence that the BMW had been repainted. Dr. Gore thought he had been defrauded by purchasing a new BMW that, unknown to him, had been repainted. Dr. Gore's BMW had incurred minimal damage to the paint during transit to the dealership. Because the cost of touching up the paint job was less than 3% of the suggested retail price, BMW, as per its written policy, sold the car as new without advising the dealer of any repainting.

The case went to trial, and the jury awarded Dr. Gore $4,000 in actual damages. The jury assessed against BMW and awarded Dr. Gore $4,000,000 in punitive damages. Think about that, $4 million because the BMW had minor paint damage. The case went to the United States Supreme Court. It overturned the punitive damages verdict on the grounds that the incredibly excessive punitive damage award violated BMW's due process rights. *BMW v. Gore* was the first time the United States Supreme Court ruled that punitive damages could be so excessive that they violate a defendant's constitutionally guaranteed due process rights.

On another front, these large punitive damage awards in Alabama were casting a bad light on the State as an unfriendly place for companies to do business. The "tort hell" moniker was not good for attracting businesses to locate in Alabama. So, the business interests began advertising campaigns against the plaintiffs' lawyers driving the incredibly large punitive damage verdicts. Moreover, Alabama Supreme Court justices who, for the most part in the early to mid-nineties, were incredibly liberal, are elected officials. The business interests got together and backed conservative justices to run for seats up for reelection. The business community did a magnificent job of stacking the Alabama Supreme Court with conservative justices. The final death knell to the crazy, large punitive damages verdicts in Alabama was the *Terminix* decision by the U.S. Supreme Court. It held arbitration provisions in contracts were valid in cases involving interstate commerce, which resulted in the ability for companies to avoid jury trials in favor of arbitration. Almost every contract involves interstate commerce. So with the trifecta of *BMW v. Gore;* a conservative, business-friendly Alabama Supreme Court; and arbitration, Alabama has never been the same.

CHAPTER ELEVEN
BECOMING A TRIAL LAWYER

Around this time, I began to change my practice. After being in the courtroom in front of judges on a consistent basis either arguing motions or at class action certification hearings, I knew I wanted to try jury cases. I was fortunate to be able to switch my area of practice to medical malpractice defense. During the nineties and throughout most of the 2000s, my firm represented physicians insured by MedMutual, the largest medical malpractice insurance carrier in Alabama. MedMutual's philosophy was great for defense lawyers who wanted to try cases. It settled cases sparingly, even some that probably should have been.

I was also fortunate to get into the medical malpractice area of the firm as lawsuits against doctors were exploding at the time. The thing about defending doctors in medical malpractice lawsuits is there are no easy ones to cut your teeth on. The first case I handled was defending a young female obstetrician in a brain damaged baby case. The mother was in labor at the hospital and suddenly suffered a ruptured uterus. The obstetrician had been called to come for a normal delivery about ten minutes before the rupture. When the obstetrician arrived in the delivery room expecting a routine delivery, the fetal heart monitor was beeping slowly, indicating a problem. Upon examination, the obstetrician found the baby's head was only at the plus one station, too high for an imminent delivery. When the obstetrician was called for delivery, the baby had been at the "plus three" station (ready to be delivered). The uterine rupture caused the baby to become partially extruded from the uterus and floating in the peritoneal cavity. This, in turn, caused oxygen deprivation and imminent brain damage.

The obstetrician tried to deliver with a vacuum but could not pull the baby out. An emergency C-section followed, but it was too late. While the baby survived, it suffered severe brain damage from lack of oxygen. In medical lingo, the baby suffered an hypoxic-ischemic encephalopathy resulting in a persistent vegetative state. In laymen's terms, the baby was a vegetable. This was not the easiest case to start with, but we had a great result as our obstetrician was dismissed before the case went to trial.

In handling medical malpractice cases, I worked with one of the best lawyers I have ever seen in my career, Norman Waldrop. Working up and trying cases with Norman really shaped my development as a defense trial lawyer. I was fortunate to learn from one of the best. The work was challenging. To properly defend a doctor, we had to learn an incredible amount of medicine. A lawyer cannot properly defend a doctor unless he fully understands the medicine. In my cases, I spent countless hours researching and reviewing medical literature, including articles and textbooks, and consulting with experts in the field. (Actually, the hours were not "countless" as I recorded them on my time sheet and billed for them). We were always incredibly prepared when the case went to trial.

Starting about 30 days out from a trial, the work was endless, working weekends and late into the night. But it was great work. The lawyers on the other side of the case were always good. Because the cost of prosecuting a medical malpractice case was so expensive, the run of the mill plaintiff lawyers couldn't afford to prosecute a medical malpractice case. Also, no good lawyers filed medical cases that had low damages. Most medical malpractice cases involved brain damage, amputation, death or worse. The stakes were high in every case we handled.

In a fairly short period of time, Norman and I tried four medical malpractice cases, losing once. The case we lost should have never gone to trial in the first place. We were defending an emergency room physician who failed to order a head CT scan on a 70-year old patient on Coumadin, a blood thinner, who had fallen and hit her head. The ER physician discharged the patient. Approximately six hours later, the patient was brought back to the emergency room in a coma. She had suffered a subdural hematoma (a brain bleed) that expanded so large it caused severe brain damage resulting in death.

The ER doctor had retired by the time the plaintiff filed the lawsuit. He was living the good life in The Villages, Florida retirement community. He wanted the case settled and over with. He bought medical malpractice insurance to resolve this exact situation. We could have settled the case before trial for under $500,000. MedMutual didn't settle. The case proceeded to trial, and we got hit for $2.1 million. We put on a hell of a defense, but the facts were just stacked against us. The codefendant hospital admitted through its witnesses at trial on several occasions that it breached the standard of care in its care and treatment of the patient. Since our client was an emergency room physician at the hospital, we simply could not separate ourselves and went down with the ship.

CHAPTER TWELVE
SHOULDER DYSTOCIA CASE: "GOING TO BLISTER YOU!"

Norman and I had some great victories. One in particular was the defense of an obstetrician in a shoulder dystocia case. Shoulder dystocia has been described as an obstetrician's nightmare as a seemingly normal delivery suddenly stops as the baby's shoulder becomes lodged under the mother's pubic bone. The first sign of a shoulder dystocia is the "turtle sign" where the baby's descent stops abruptly and the head retracts back like a turtle's head in the shell. The obstetrician has only minutes to deliver the baby before blood flow to the baby's brain is restricted enough to cause brain damage. The problem is the baby's shoulder is stuck and the baby will not come out.

The standard of care requires the obstetrician to perform certain recognized maneuvers to release the shoulder and complete the delivery. The first maneuver is always the "McRoberts" maneuver where the nurses or doctor holds the mother's legs back and at the same time applies pressure to the pubic area in an attempt to increase the space for delivery and dislodge the shoulder. If that technique is unsuccessful, additional maneuvers can be used, including attempting to turn the baby (known as the Woods' corkscrew maneuver) to release the impacted shoulder. Another method involves intentionally breaking the clavicle if the shoulder will not release. If nothing works, the last resort is the "Zavanelli" maneuver. This is where the obstetrician calls for an emergency C-section and shoves the baby back up into the uterus and surgically removes the baby through the incision. If the Zavanelli is required, the outcome is typically poor.

The obstetrician must not attempt to pull the baby out using too much force. If the doctor tries to pull the baby out, the result can be an Erb's palsy where the nerve roots in the shoulder are pulled away from the spinal cord. The physics of this are simple: as the head is pulled and the shoulder does not move, the nerve roots get stretched until they are torn. The result can be permanent paralysis of the arm.

We tried a shoulder dystocia Erb's palsy case where the child's right arm was permanently paralyzed. In our case, after the shoulder dystocia was noted, the obstetrician performed the McRoberts maneuver and delivered the baby. The shoulder dystocia seemed fairly uncomplicated. Unfortunately, during the delivery, the baby's nerve roots in his right shoulder and neck area, known as the brachial plexus, were torn away from the spinal cord, resulting in paralysis of the arm. I never thought the obstetrician breached the standard of care. He did the correct maneuvers and delivered the baby. There was just an unfortunate result.

I worked the case up and retained fantastic expert witnesses, one of whom was an author of *Williams on Obstetrics* - the obstetrician's bible. The trial took a week. The plaintiff was represented by a hotshot lawyer out of Miami who demanded $6 million to settle the case prior to trial. The Miami lawyer told me before trial when we refused to settle, *"We're going to blister you at trial!"* I gave the opening statement and cross examined the child's parents and plaintiff's damage experts. I gave the first 20 minutes of closing argument (my first closing). When I sat back down at counsel table after my close, our doctor leaned over and whispered, "Great job."

The Miami lawyer made a big mistake by bringing the child in to the courtroom for the jury to observe. The child was about 4 years old by the time of trial. He could not move his right arm, but he was incredibly active, laughing, and running around the courtroom. The kid looked great. You didn't feel sorry for him. The jury returned a defense verdict after deliberating only 15 minutes. After the verdict, the Miami lawyer told me: *"I've never had my ass kicked so badly."*

CHAPTER THIRTEEN
WORKING ON MY CRAFT

I learned to become a very good trial lawyer by working with and watching Norman. I was not just a "briefcase carrier." Not only did I primarily work the cases up to prepare them for trial, I always took a significant role at the trial. I typically gave the opening statement and always cross examined the family members of the dead or injured patient. I developed the skill of being kind and sympathetic while extracting the necessary information from family members. Too often family members gave testimony at trial over exaggerating the plaintiff's poor condition or testified to events that they claimed to have witnessed at the hospital that were not supported by the facts – the typical "gilding of the lily." This testimony was always unnecessary and didn't help their case. It actually hurt the plaintiff's case once the jury realized after my cross that their testimony was at the least exaggerated, if not just untrue. Juries tend to not award money to people they believe are bullshitting them.

Being a trial lawyer has allowed me some wonderful experiences. Nothing beats the thrill of trying a case in front of a jury. When I was a young lawyer, I heard older trial lawyers say that trying a case is the most fun you can have indoor with your clothes on. That statement could not be more true. The rush after winning a case is indescribable. Putting two years of work into a case and coming out on top gave me a similar feeling to winning a football or basketball game. Winning is exhilarating, losing is devastating. The competitive drive and desire to win I developed during my abbreviated athletic career were stoked by courtroom battles. Trying cases did not match athletic competition, but it was close.

But one thing I've found during my career is that no matter how good the lawyer is, the lawyer does not control the facts of the case. What makes really great lawyers are really great facts. Very few times in my career have I seen a lawyer's skill in trying a case overcome bad facts.

Specializing in medical malpractice defense work had two great advantages. First, typically most of the medical malpractice cases filed go to trial. For any defense lawyer wanting to try cases, medical malpractice defense was the best option. On the flip side, approximately 95% of all other cases settle and never get to trial. There is a major difference in being a litigator versus a trial lawyer. Until you see how pre-trial litigation efforts come together in an actual trial, you really have no idea what you are doing as a lawyer.

There are lawyers practicing in the biggest firms in the world who do nothing but handle discovery in lawsuits. These lawyers never try cases but jump from case to case just taking depositions. Depositions are when lawyers take pretrial testimony from witnesses and parties under oath. Deposition testimony is crucial to winning cases at trial. Cross examination at trial comes from deposition testimony. The rule of thumb is never ask a question on cross to which you don't already know the answer. You also ask only leading questions on cross. You never ask an open ended question on cross that would give an adverse witness the chance to explain or expound upon his or her answer. The questions and answers on cross have already been established by deposition testimony.

If a witness at trial gives a different answer to a question asked at deposition, the lawyer can crush the witness by referring to the deposition testimony and pointing out to the jury how the witness gave prior sworn testimony different than that given at trial. I love it when a witness gives trial testimony contradictory to deposition testimony. Typically, a witness will only do this once during a trial because I make them look so bad when I show the jury the prior testimony.

The point to all of this is: if all a lawyer does is piecemeal discovery work in hundreds of cases and has no idea of trial strategy from the beginning, the depositions taken by that lawyer are just a discovery crap shoot. I'm already looking to trial and have formed a preliminary trial strategy before I take the first deposition. I know the issues in the case. Taking a deposition is not just preparing a bunch of question and reading off that script, it is understanding the case and thinking ahead on how you will use the transcript from the deposition at trial.

Second, medical malpractice cases are typically easier to win than other types of cases, especially for doctors, not so much for hospitals. Juries, at least in Alabama, want to give a doctor the benefit of the doubt. Of course, some venues are worse than others. Mobile County is a tough place to win any case for a defendant. A percentage of the population in Mobile County is poor and uneducated. This leads to most Mobile County juries having a representative percentage of poor, uneducated jurors. In general, these kind of jurors favor plaintiffs and award larger damages. That's not being prejudiced, it's just the facts. Take Shelby County, on the other hand. Shelby County is a fairly affluent county south of Birmingham. Plaintiff's lawyers would rather not try cases in Shelby County. Affluent and well-educated people just make better defense jurors. The statistics bear that out.

In every medical malpractice case that goes to trial, the lawyers for the doctor will have expert witnesses who practice in the same field as the doctor being sued. These expert witnesses testify that the doctor's care and treatment of the patient met the standard of care. Typically, the experts retained by defense lawyers are tops in their field, widely published, and teach at major university medical centers. As often as I can, I retain experts from the University of Alabama at Birmingham ("UAB"), one of the top medical institutions in the world. A UAB doctor has a lot of influence over an Alabama jury.

If a defense lawyer can't find a qualified expert to support the doctor's case, which is rare, the case will typically settle. So, most of the time, defensible cases were the ones tried, resulting in trial victories. Because of this built in bias toward being successful in trying medical malpractice cases, medical malpractice lawyers win a larger percentage of their trials than lawyers in other fields.

Trying cases and becoming known as a trial lawyer is a badge of honor in the legal profession. One of my biggest pet peeves (other than the word "pet peeve" itself - I hate that word) has always been that plaintiff lawyers refer to themselves collectively as "trial lawyers." Most lawyers that are "litigators," plaintiff or defendant, at least profess they want to try cases. My sense though has been when push comes to shove, a lot of litigators are glad when their cases settle without having to lace up the wing-tips and get it on at trial. But I digress. The plaintiffs' bar has adopted and promoted itself as "trial lawyers." But who do the "trial lawyers" try their cases against? Other "trial lawyers," of course, who happen to be defense lawyers. In every case a plaintiff sues a defendant, and in every resulting trial, the plaintiff's lawyer tries his case against a defense lawyer. So in every case ever tried in the United States, defense lawyers have tried just as many cases as plaintiff lawyers - it's 50-50.

CHAPTER FOURTEEN
TRYING A CASE IN HARPER LEE'S HOMETOWN

One of the most memorable cases Norman and I tried was defending a physician in the small, country town of Monroeville, Alabama. A mother, 28 weeks pregnant, came to the hospital after suffering a placental abruption. The doctor did not perform a C-section at the time because he believed he found the baby's heartbeat on the fetal heart monitor. The mother remained in the hospital overnight, and in the morning, the physician aborted the fetus when he realized the fetus was not alive. We showed at trial that what the doctor was picking up on the fetal heart monitor was actually the mother's heartbeat and argued the fetus had actually died prior to the mother reaching the hospital. Even though the doctor mistakenly believed the fetus was alive and did not attempt immediate delivery, which arguably was a breach of the standard of care, the mistake had no effect on the outcome because the fetus was already dead.

The case tried for almost two weeks. At one point during the trial, the defendant doctor became so angry at the plaintiff's lawyer during cross examination that he came off the witness stand to punch the plaintiff's lawyer. The doctor had been practicing in Monroeville for over 30 years. He had delivered over 2,000 babies. Monroeville was his home. He was well-known and well-respected in the community. He did not like it when a lawyer from Mobile came up to Monroeville to criticize him. I can't recall the exact question on cross that got the doctor so mad that he came unglued. It may have been the smart-ass, snarky tone of the questions. There was questioning about the doctor leaving the hospital in the middle of the night to rest and eat a sandwich while his patient lied in the hospital bleeding and her fetus dead. Of course, since it was cross-examination, it was not so much questioning, but the plaintiff's lawyer making derogatory statements followed by, *"Isn't that right, doctor?"* This was the first and only time in my career I have ever seen a witness become so angry he left the witness stand to fight the lawyer crossing him. Norman jumped up and got in between the doctor and the plaintiff's lawyer. After a short recess, the cross examination continued.

knows about your disability. I was talking with a girl in a bar while in law school. She was pretty, smart, and funny. Seemed perfect. She and some of her friends had come up to a table where my friends and I had already been sitting. She had no idea who I was. I asked her for her number. She eagerly gave it to me and said I better call her. It was going great. Eventually, I got up to leave and she saw me walk for the first time. I didn't think anything about it. I called her the next day. I never got a call back. The lesson: you can't surprise (or shock) someone who takes an interest in you. I learned not to start down the road of "courting" without full disability disclosure.

There certainly have been women that would not want a relationship with someone with such an apparent disability. And I understand that. I would not want to date someone who walked as oddly as I do. Being with someone else who walks the way I do would just be too much. There has to be some balance in a relationship and I walk weirdly enough for two people.

CHAPTER SIXTEEN
SORRY FOR THE DIGRESSION: BACK TO THE STORY

Back to the marriage discussion. To make matters more strained, we started having kids right away. Because Tam was 33 when we got married, she wanted to go ahead and start a family. Tam was pregnant within two months of our wedding. Within our first three years of marriage, we had two boys. Cullen was born on March 25, 1994 and Connor was born on July 7, 1995. So here we were, a couple who had been married for three years, who did not even really know each other, with two small children and me working constantly. Looking back on it, it is all a blur. Our daughter Corbit was born on March 5, 1998.

Tam and I have been married 25 years. Not bad for a couple who probably may not have married had we dated longer. This doesn't mean one of us is good and the other bad. It simply means our personalities are so different that we may have had more peaceful and tranquil marriages with other people. I'm proud of our marriage lasting this long. I expect it to last until one of us dies. Though she can drive me nuts, I love my wife dearly.

Tam is fairly rule-oriented and unbending. I've always been pretty laid back. If we were ever going to get divorced, it would have been in those early years. At the time Corbit was born, Cullen was almost four and Connor not even three. One thing Tam and I both have in common is a strong work ethic. She managed the house and did an incredibly wonderful job taking care of our children when they were young. There was considerable stress back in those days. I was traveling on a regular basis - not the glamourous travel, but road trips covering hearings in courthouses throughout the State. My work hours were long. Tam's were longer. It was always fun to walk in the door after a 12-hour day to be greeted at the door with Tam holding Corbit, Cullen and Connor running wild in the house, and having Tam hand me Corbit and say, "It's your turn." The truth is, she was exhausted.

Even though I was working extremely long hours at the time, I was a very hands-on father. I changed my share of diapers, which is actually pretty difficult when your left hand

CHAPTER SEVENTEEN
THE DAY MY HEART BROKE

The most painful experience of my life has come during my role as a father. You love your kids so much, and it kills you when they hurt. During Connor's freshman year at Auburn, he got sick with really bad congestion. He started having horrible pain in his right eye. He went to the campus medical clinic and was immediately sent to the local hospital. The pressure in his eye was unbearable. His eye was swollen shut. It was shortly after lunch when Tam told me what was going on. I spoke to the doctor at the hospital who was extremely concerned about Connor's eye. I starting driving from Mobile to the hospital near Auburn. Just south of Montgomery, the doctor called me and said Connor needed to see an eye specialist immediately, and he had arranged for Life Flight to fly Connor to UAB. So, instead of turning onto I-85 toward Auburn when I hit Montgomery, I kept going north toward Birmingham.

I arrived at UAB as Connor's helicopter was landing. I first saw him in the ER. His right eye was so swollen, he was almost unrecognizable. An ophthalmology resident was testing Connor's right eye with what looked like an old View-Master. Connor was moaning in pain. The resident took me out in the hallway and explained the infection causing Connor's congestion had travelled to his right eye. The eye was swollen so badly, no blood could leave his eye, which meant no new blood could enter his eye. With no oxygenation to his eye, his eye basically died. He told me Connor most likely would never regain sight in his right eye. I had never heard of something like this, even with all the medical cases I had handled. It took me several minutes just to process what the doctor had told me. This couldn't be right.

The nurses gave Connor some pain medicine that knocked him out. They admitted Connor to the hospital and transferred him to a room. Connor was out most of the night. I sat in a chair in his room completely devastated. The next morning, the attending ophthalmologist assessed Connor and confirmed to me what the resident told me the previous night. I didn't want Connor to learn for the first time he would be forever blind in his right eye from a doctor. I needed to tell him. I tried to be strong, but couldn't get the words out before breaking down. I've never hurt so badly, ever. I finally choked out the explanation as to what happened and the prognosis. Connor took it better than I did.

To make matters worse, Connor's right eye wasn't moving so he looked like he had a lazy eye. So, not only had this kid lost his sight in his right eye, he had to deal with the cosmetic defect. He was in the hospital for 5 days. He came home wearing a patch. Two days later, he returned to Auburn to resume classes. His eye was still red and swollen. Cullen and I went to see him the following weekend. We went to see Auburn play Georgia in basketball, ate some Mexican food, and hung out for a while. Connor was pretty down. I hated leaving. I wanted to just take him home, but I knew staying on campus was the best thing for him.

After 3 weeks or so, the swelling was gone. I was hoping for a miracle, but didn't get one. Connor will never see out of his right eye again. He has handled it incredibly well. Actually, his life has not changed at all. He has never felt sorry for himself. There is nothing he doesn't do now that he did before. He played all the intramural sports. He loves to golf. He's just taken it all in stride and I'm so proud of him. Maybe I was a good role model on how to handle adversity. Connor's tougher than I am. The minor miracle is that Connor's right eye began moving in sync with his left eye. You can't even tell Connor is blind in his right eye. Sometimes I even have to remind myself he can't see out of his right eye.

tripped while walking and holding Cullen as an infant, we decided it was probably best for me not to carry the kids around.

Tam is pretty tough. She has never made me feel bad about not being able to do physically demanding chores around the house. She matter of factly goes about her business. When you throw in doing the laundry, cooking, cleaning and other typical housewife tasks on top of everything else she does, the only conclusion I have ever reached is Tam is pretty extraordinary.

As we grow old together, I'm going to be the one who benefits most. I know my body will start falling apart long before hers. I joke that when I'm sixty, I'm going to walk around with a football helmet and hip pads so I won't suffer a brain bleed or break a hip when I fall. Tam is a classic beauty. Although six years older than me, she will age gracefully. Actually, she keeps getting better looking. I tell her by the time she's eighty, she will look incredible. Our 25-year marriage, although not perfect, when you throw in raising our kids together and where we are as a family, has been pretty great.

Emporia, Virginia – Dixie Youth All-Stars. (1978)

That's me, number 35. Eighth grade. Obviously, before the longer shorts became popular. (1980)

One of the only football action shots I have. Running with the ball in junior high, one year before my injury. (1980) Favorite number, 17.

OPERATIVE NOTE

(this is your copy)

CATE, RODNEY REED
78 16 95
P/Dr. McWhorter
Date of Operation: 8-15-81

CLEAN CASE

PREOPERATIVE DIAGNOSIS: Cervical fracture with spinal cord injury.

OPERATION: Cervical laminectomy, C4, and cervical fusion, C3, 4, 5, and 6.

SURGEON: Dr. McWhorter.

ASSISTANTS: Drs. Buehler and Branch.

RESIDENT CODE: I.

ANESTHESIA: General endotracheal using Halothane, Anectine, Pavulon, Nitrous Oxide, Oxygen.

ANESTHETISTS: Mullinax, Huffstetler, Hanes, and Dr. Tolmie.

OPERATIVE TIME: 2 hours and 45 minutes.

A portion of my operative note. I've read hundreds of these defending physicians. Somewhat surreal to read my own, especially the clinical summery. (1981)

CLINICAL SUMMARY: This 15-year-old white male was injured playing football yesterday, and became quadriplegic. He has on X-ray a compression fracture of C4 with some evidence of instability, and also fractured pedicle in line of C4. He had a myelogram performed which showed a total block at the C4 area. He is brought to the Operating Room at this time for cervical laminectomy.

A picture from the newspaper capturing my first return to South Stokes, and my first taste of freedom from rehab. With me is my friend Larry Hartle who remains one of my closest friends. (1981)

This picture was taken shortly after I returned to high school. Face still puffy from the steriods. Hair growing back out. Pictured with my brother, Mike. (1981)

Me with my law school roommate and great friend, George Podgorny at a Mardi Gras party in Chapel Hill, NC. (1989)

Davidson College graduation. Mike, mom, and me. (1988)

At my sister Lisa's wedding with my brother, Mike, and our dad. (1989)

Me in front of the Taj Mahal. What an experience. (2012)

The Chhatrapati Shivaji Terminus in Mumbai, India. The most architecturally stunning building I have ever seen. (2012)

My best friend in high school Larry Hartle, me, Larry's sons Zach and Josh, at Lenior Rhyne College in Hickory, NC. I'm 6'2" and seldom one of the shortest guys in a photo. Zach played basketball at Tusculum University. This photo was taken after a game. (2016)

Cullen and I in Maggie Valley, NC at a cabin we like to rent in the winter. Maggie Valley is one of my favorite places in the world. (2016)

Cullen, Connor, Tam and I at Sky Bar in Auburn, AL. Sky Bar is one of the "most Ubered" to locations in Alabama. Great bar. (2016)

My 50th birthday trip to Costa Rica with Davidson College friends – me, Art Stitzer, David Lilley and my brother Mike. (2016)

Cullen and I at the Incredible Christmas Place in Pigeon Forge, TN. (2016)

Family photo time – me, Tam, Corbit, Cullen and Connor. (2016)

Corbit and I getting ready to ride the Lightening Rod at Dollywood. The world's fastest wooden rollercoaster. Top speed of 73 mph. (2016)

Me in front of the Cub's dugout. Took the tour of Wrigley Field. Cubs fan since 1984 when cable TV first came to King, NC. Started watching the Cubs on WGN. (2017)

Some of my best friends from Davidson College – Steve Judge, me, David Lilley, Harry Schiavi and Gat Caperton. Picture taken at the New Belgium Brewery in Asheville, NC. Went to the North Carolina mountains for David's 50th birthday and to see the eclipse. (2017)

The crew in Pigeon Forge, Tennessee – Cullen, me, my mom, Connor, my niece Nicole, my sister Lisa and my brother-in-law Mark. (2017)

Photo taken during a long weekend trip to Don's cabin in the Wisconsin North Woods – Pat Gloor, Don Ivansek and I at Bent's Camp, Land 'O' Lakes, Wisconsin. (2017)

Tam and I at Café Negril on Frenchmen Street in New Orleans. One of our favorite bars. Also check out Blue Nile and 30°/ 90° on Frenchmen Street. (2018)

We can't use the term "midget," because it is offensive, but instead must use the term "little people." Like that is less offensive? I get how the term "dwarf" is a bit offensive as it connotes the seven dwarves. But "midget?" Come on. I love the scene in *"Elf"* when Will Ferrell's character Buddy the Elf, bursts into a meeting where a "little person" is pitching ideas for a children's book and Buddy innocently asks the little person, *"Does Santa know you left the workshop?"* Of course, that is so offensive it's hilarious.

It's no different for the handicapped. I guess I should not speak for all the handicapped, but there needs to be a little lightening up. I refer to myself as a "handi," for no other reason than it is short for handicapped. (Just this second when I typed that sentence, I realized a 'handi" is short for a hand-job. Damn, now I'm going to have to find another word.) I don't take offense if someone refers to me as disabled or handicapped. I'm not a big fan of "crippled" because that word, at least for me, paints the picture of someone old, feeble, and miserable. But again, it's just a word.

Because of my gait and the difficulty in lifting my left foot off the ground when I walk, I occasionally stub my toe, trip, and fall. Sometimes I trip and fall once every six months. Sometimes I will trip and fall three times in one week. Falling is frustrating, embarrassing, and worst of all, it hurts. Sometimes I trip and fall because I am not paying attention. Most of the time though, it's because I stubbed my left toe. A normal person can stub his toe but recover before falling down. I typically can't. My muscles won't move quickly enough to recover once I lose my balance. I've got a chance if it is a left toe stub because my right leg is stronger and easier to move. If I can get it under me, I can regain my balance. If I have the rare right toe stub, I have no chance. There's no way I'm going to pick up my left foot to save myself from falling. I go down fast and hard.

I've developed a talent for falling the right way over the years. It has taken a long time to learn how to properly fall to minimize injury. Darwinian survival of the fittest for the handicapped. The typical fall happens like this: I stub my left toe. My body begins leaning forward and I get to the point where I know I cannot recover. When I know I am going to hit the ground I get this "oh shit" feeling and I know there is nothing I can do. Then comes the feeling of helplessness where my mind knows what's coming but I physically can do nothing to prevent it. Following that is almost an electrical shock that goes through my body as my entire body stiffens. Then the fall itself happens. When I fall, I drop like a tree that has been cut down. My upper body starts tilting toward the ground. There is typically a one to two second feeling of "crap, this sucks" as the ground comes rushing up to my face.

The body's normal reaction to falling is to attempt to break the fall by putting out your hands - big mistake. What I have learned to do over time is to ball up my fists and put my forearms right below my neck to attempt to cushion the blow of what is usually an extremely hard surface. It took some time to master this falling position since it is not a natural reflex. I've learned this after breaking my left ring finger three times from falls. When I fall, the muscles controlling my left ring finger for some reason bend the finger downward. In the past, when I would catch my body weight with this left hand, my left finger would be caught underneath my left hand and snap right below the fingernail. Each time, the same result. I would not even realize I had broken my finger until I was attempting to get up and looked at my left hand and the end of my left ring finger would be pointed straight downward with the nail ripped out of the bed at the base and blood everywhere. So each time this happened, I drove to the emergency room to get my finger fixed.

One perk of defending doctors is I never wait in the emergency room. I usually know at least one ER doctor working the day shift. The fix was the same each time. First the shots of Marcaine to numb my finger. Then the doctor forced my nail back under the skin at the base and pulled the skin over the nail at which time the skin was sewed to connect the nail. Then a cautery was used to place two holes in my nail so that any blood underneath could escape and not build up pressure to dislodge the nail. I would then get a small plastic brace to put on the end of my finger, get taped up and head back to work.

Falling sucks. Any sense of coolness I believe I possess disappears when I fall. But, I've accepted falling as part of the deal of being fortunate to be able to walk. I know this is a cliché, but it's not the number of times I fall that matters, it's the number of times I get back up. As long as these two numbers equal, I'm okay.

As difficult as it is for me to walk, I walk quite a bit. Not as much over the past few years. I do not enjoy walking from point A to point B when I have to be somewhere in a certain amount of time. I do enjoy walking when I have time to stop, take my time, look around, and enjoy what I'm doing. For instance, I'm fine walking a long way in a museum or an art gallery where I am walking, stopping, looking at things, and moving on. For someone who has some paralysis from the neck down, I'm quite active physically. I've played golf. I've done the "physically challenged" assisted snow skiing. I bowl. I've driven snowmobiles. I've zip-lined. I trout fish in the mountains, which requires scaling riverbanks. I usually finish a fishing trip in the mountains with cuts, scrapes, and bruises all over my legs from getting up and down steep riverbanks.

It's been over 35 years since my accident. I can't remember what it was like to walk normally. I certainly cannot recall what it was like to run. I exercise everyday unless I am out of town. Exercising is probably the most enjoyable activity I do each day. I'm up at 4:30 in the morning, drink a glass of Spark, and hit the gym. I get on the elliptical machine, which simulates a running motion, and get going pretty good. Once gravity is taken away, it is a lot easier for me to move my legs and move them rapidly. I've had so many people come up to me while I am working out to tell me what an inspiration I am to them and watching me exercise the way I do gives them the motivation to exercise. My typical response, which is the truth, is that I am no inspiration. I am just a guy who is doing what it takes to get through and enjoy life. There really is no choice but to attempt to live life as normally as possible. Exercising and being in the best shape I can be in is just something I have to do. Oftentimes, when I am flying to a meeting or a deposition, I will have a conversation with someone at the gate or on the plane who has seen me walk. When they find out that I am a lawyer, a lot of times they are in disbelief, not expecting that somebody who walks the way I do could have such a profession.

Everyone has issues and problems. Mine are just more apparent than others.

CHAPTER TWENTY
GUESS MY CONDITION

The exchange typically goes like this:

"MS?"

"Excuse me?"

"Do you have MS?"

These inquiries into my condition happen much more than I would have ever expected. Total strangers I see walking on the street, in and out of buildings, or wherever, will just come up to me and basically ask what's wrong with me. I have become accustomed to young children staring at me when they walk by me. I think that's natural for children to be inquisitive when they see me walking.

It has never particularly bothered me when I get the "guess the condition" questions from total strangers. I am always friendly when I respond. The problem is I then feel the need to explain my condition and what happened, which then typically begins a drawn out conversation that I really have no interest in having. I have no problem talking about my condition and what led to it with friends or even strangers in a situation where I'm not going somewhere and have time to discuss it.

I guess when a stranger stops me on the street to ask me if I have MS, I could just say *"no"* and keep moving, but that would appear to be rude. I would assume if I just answer the question *"no"* the follow-up question would be *"so, what is your condition?"*

I have had complete strangers not only ask me if I have MS, but also cerebral palsy, polio or if I've had a stroke. The stroke question came when Cullen and I were at the beach. We were trying to get out of the surf and back to our beach chairs when a wave took us both down. I typically stay out of the ocean unless the waves are calm. I love swimming in the ocean and the feel of saltwater on me after getting out. One of the most difficult things for me to do is trying to get out of the surf. Waves hit me from behind while at the same time the surf is moving in the opposite direction. It is impossible to balance. It usually takes two people, one on each arm, to get me back on to the beach. Getting out in the surf is probably a stupid thing for me to do. I swim pretty well for someone with residual quadriplegia, but not well enough to handle a rip current.

So, on this occasion when I got knocked down by the surf, an older guy came out to help. We got up and another wave took all of us down again. I started laughing so hard I almost choked on sea water. I was thinking how ridiculous I must have looked trying to get out of the surf and the three of us getting knocked down. I've gotten to the place where I don't think about how I look when I attempt physical activities I probably shouldn't. Otherwise, I would be too embarrassed to try anything. After we made it safely to the beach, the older guy that helped me asked me if I had suffered a stroke. I said, *"no."* He proceeded to tell me about his stroke and his recovery. We talked for another 10 minutes. I figured I owed him at least that.

Nine times out of ten after I respond to the what is your condition question, the strangers respond with their own story about themselves, a relative or a friend who has the condition about which they asked. So, as I am walking somewhere, I get to listen to a story about a friend or relative of a complete stranger and their condition. The conversation usually ends with the stranger telling me that I'm doing just great. Now I can get on with my day.

I certainly don't want to speak on behalf of all handicapped people, but I think as a general rule, it might be a good idea to not come up to a person you don't know who is clearly handicapped and ask that person what is wrong with him. I could not imagine going up to someone I don't know who walks strangely and ask him, *"Do you have (fill in condition)?"*

Now, when I meet a new client for the first time, I always work into the initial conversation what happened to me. I can imagine a doctor facing a lawsuit, meeting his lawyer for the first time and seeing me walking down the hall thinking, *"What the hell?"* I have never had any problem with any physician questioning my ability because of my physical limitations. And when I think back on that, it is somewhat surprising that clients have accepted me 100% of the time without question. I have never even had to explain or assure a client that I am able to defend him or her and perform all the necessary litigation activities even with my limited physical abilities. Actually, in most of my cases, I become very good friends with my doctor clients by the time the case is over.

If I were to ever write a book on *"how not to treat the handicapped,"* I would include this story: While out with Cullen (20 years old at the time) and one of my friends, at the dog track of all places, an employee of the dog track asked me in front of my friend and son, *"How long have you been struggling to walk like that?"* So, we have a total stranger pointing out how strangely I walk in front of my son and friend, and then asking me to engage in a conversation with him to explain the history of my condition. I tried to brush it off by saying something to the effect of, *"Oh, it's a long story,"* and attempted to ignore him. He then launched into his story about a friend of his who had a son with cerebral palsy who walked just like me but had gotten used to walking that way and could walk so fast with crutches and even though it looked like with every step he was going to fall, he never did. Wow! How do you respond to that? Fortunately, after his story, he went about his business. I just looked at my friend and son, shook my head and we continued to enjoy our day.

CHAPTER TWENTY-ONE
MY THOUGHTS ON RELIGION

If asked, I say I'm a Christian. But I have serious belief issues and doubts. I try to believe in God and in Jesus, but my mind won't allow me to readily accept their existence.

Wouldn't it be something if there actually is no God, not only with regard to Christianity but in any religion? Think of all the killing that has occurred over the centuries in the name of religion: the Christian martyrs, the Crusades, the killing of Jews by Hitler, radical Islam - kill all the infidels - all for nothing.

I cannot square evolution, dinosaurs, and probable life on other planets in this vast universe with the Bible. It's hard for me to believe that all humans and non-fish animals were destroyed by a great flood and the only surviving humans and animals were contained in Noah's ark and repopulated the entire world. My family and I do not go to church very often. I am a member of a Wednesday morning men's group that meets at the church. I feel somewhat hypocritical as most members of the group, about 40 of us, are devout Christians and bigtime believers. We start the Wednesday morning group at 5:30 a.m. We all meet together for about 45 minutes when one member puts on a presentation. After the presentation and voicing of prayer concerns, we split into small groups of five to ten people. I do enjoy my small group. Over the years, we have become extremely close. Most men, as opposed to women, do not have a close-knit group of friends with whom to unload problems, seek advice, and just talk for about an hour once a week. The small group gives me the opportunity to talk about any issues or problems going on in my life with a close-knit group of guys who also talk about their problems. For any guys reading this, I highly recommend finding a small group of guys in whom you can confide and discuss problems going on in your life.

I've read and studied the Bible more during the past five years of my life than I ever have. I've read the Gospels and the Letters of Paul. I am a fan of the New Testament. Not so much of the Old Testament. The Old Testament God is spiteful and vengeful. The difference I see in the Old Testament God and the New Testament God is that in the New Testament there is value placed on every person's life. In the Old Testament, God smites hundreds of people without a second thought.

Whether you believe in God or Jesus, the New Testament provides a very good instruction manual on how to live your life: love God with all your heart and love your neighbors as yourself. Basically, live by the Golden Rule. Proverbs is very well written and gives great advice on how to live.

My problem with the New Testament is it seems to me much of it is written to give hope to the poor, oppressed, struggling, etc. by promising them this world is fleeting and they will be the ones living the good life in heaven. It's as if the New Testament was written for the downtrodden so they would accept their plight in life without rebellion because they are promised a spot in heaven. Another problem I have with the New Testament is the Letters of Paul. There is constant discussion of how Jesus' return to earth is imminent. Paul clearly believed Jesus' return would be weeks or months. These letters were written by Paul more than 2,000 years ago. I could not imagine anyone who read these letters or heard Paul and/or the apostles preaching about the return of Jesus would have ever thought Jesus would not have returned within the next 2,000 years.

Another problem I have with religion in general is the whole prayer thing. During our Wednesday morning men's group, before we break into small groups, we have prayer concerns and then we say a prayer. As an aside, it is amazing how many real problems people face in this life. When I listen to the prayer concerns, I hear so many families struggling with illness, cancer, and death. When I hear all these problems with which other families are struggling, it really makes me feel fortunate not to have those issues going on in my life. Having to walk with a cane is nothing compared to a mother of three kids being diagnosed with inoperable brain cancer or an active father losing a leg because of a horrible infection. If prayer does work, praying for good health is what you should focus on.

Back to prayer itself. We pray to God for healing, for jobs, for relationships to improve, for miracles. When we pray for something that actually happens, we praise God because He has answered our prayers. But, if the prayer does not come to fruition, we say it was God's will. In other words, if we pray for the healing of someone with cancer, and after the radiation and chemotherapy, the cancer goes into remission, the prayers worked. If the cancer treatment does not work, then it was God's will that this person is going to die of cancer. Really?

If there is a God, I do not believe God micromanages our lives. I hear so often if something goes wrong or badly, for instance losing a job and being unemployed, that *"God has it under control. He has a plan for you. He will provide."* I just don't think God is a headhunter placing every Christian in the world in the right job.

I do not believe God had a hand in my accident. Nor do I believe God had a hand in my recovery. If there is a God, I believe what He does is gives you strength to deal with trials you face. For those interested, see the Book of James.

If there is a heaven, I doubt I am getting in. According to the New Testament, all you have to do to get into heaven is to believe that Jesus Christ is our savior and died for our sins. In other words, you have to be saved. Once you do this, you've punched your ticket to heaven. Unfortunately for me, I have a mind that won't allow me to accept this, no matter how hard I try. Another problem I have with the Christian philosophy is no matter how many times a person sins, as long as the person asks for forgiveness, that person is back on the heaven track. At some point if you continue to sin, you become a crappy person. A crappy person shouldn't go to heaven. But as long as the crappy person keeps asking for forgiveness, supposedly, that person receives a clean slate each time and is eligible for heaven.

So a husband can cheat on his wife ten times but as long as he asks for forgiveness of his sins, he makes it into heaven. However, the guy who was faithful to his wife and a great moral and kind person who unfortunately has doubts about Jesus actually being the son of God does not make it into heaven. It doesn't hold up.

To me, Christianity is somewhat of an elitist religion. Although, I guess all religions are elitist. A true Christian is one who believes the only way to heaven is through Jesus Christ. Therefore, Jews, Muslims, Buddhists, or any person who believes in any religion other than Christianity, cannot go to heaven, no matter how great that person might be. Seems a bit arrogant. And here's the deal: to me, you can't pick and choose the parts of Christianity that fit your lifestyle and ignore the others and be a true Christian. For example, the book of Romans unequivocally states homosexuality is deviant, unacceptable behavior. I have no issue with the gay community. If someone is gay, that's fine with me. But my feelings are squarely against what the Bible says. With religion, my thought is you either have to be all in or all out.

I am envious of those who have a strong faith, no matter what their religion. I wish my mind worked that way. If there is a God, why won't He allow me to blindly believe? And the problem is I can't fake it. I can tell everybody I am a believer. Go to church every Sunday. Even preach on the street corner. Assuming God is all-knowing, He knows at the end of the day no matter what great Christian things I could ever do, my mind still won't let me believe. None of us gets out of here alive. So, I guess at some point, if there is a Christian God, I will deal with the consequences.

CHAPTER TWENTY-TWO
THE BUSINESS OF LAWYERING

Over the past five to ten years the practice of law in Mobile, Alabama has changed. Having enough work to do was never an issue. I can recall as a young associate being told not to worry about developing my own practice because the firm had so much work. Billing hours was much more important than client development. That advice could not have been more wrong. Around ten years ago, there began to be consolidation of large regional firms in the southeast. Firms from New Orleans, Atlanta, and Birmingham began gobbling up 20 to 40-person firms. The Mobile legal market was not spared this consolidation. So what happened was these regional firms were taking the work that typically would go to traditional Mobile firms because the regional firms that were counsel for large corporations now have a presence in Mobile. My firm still has several great clients, but the market has become incredibly competitive. Marketing and client development have become just as or more important than actually performing good legal work. It's tough out there.

Not only has the competition for clients become extremely fierce, the number of lawsuits being filed in Alabama has decreased. Back in the 1990s, during the tort hell years, everybody, plaintiff lawyers and defense lawyers, was making money. As the Alabama Supreme Court became more conservative, the good plaintiff's lawyers began filing national cases elsewhere. The good plaintiff's lawyers are still making money in mass tort actions, but they file lawsuits in plaintiff-friendly venues outside of Alabama and consolidate their cases in those venues. So the high quality mass tort work has left the State.

Another huge problem in Alabama, and also in other states, has been the rise of the television commercial plaintiff lawyer. It's amazing how cheesy these commercials are. Apparently, though, they work. In general, the television commercial plaintiff lawyers are not the best lawyers. They seldom actually try any cases. Several could not find their way to the courthouse. They oftentimes settle their cases pre-suit and take settlements for their clients that are only a fraction of what the clients deserve. I've been told by some of my insurance clients that the rise of the TV lawyers has been great because the insurance companies are able to settle a lot of their cases for lower amounts than they have in the past. The problem for defense lawyers is because so many of these cases are settled pre-suit, the amount of litigation has dwindled.

Most litigation work derives from insurance companies' insureds getting sued. For instance, much of my work is defending doctors in malpractice cases. A medical malpractice insurance company insures these doctors. When a doctor gets sued, the insurance company hires the lawyer to represent the doctor. A lawyer obtains and keeps legal work that derives from insurance companies by forming, building, and strengthening relationships with the decision makers who select counsel for insured defendants. Achieving good results is the best way to keep clients. A lawyer who makes an insurance adjustor look good is usually going to be successful in keeping clients.

What happens, though, is these decision makers oftentimes move from insurance company to insurance company. When a new decision maker who hires lawyers fills the position of the one that left, that person typically has built relationships with legal counsel at his prior job. So, when the insurance company decision maker leaves, the new person will want to use the lawyers he or she is comfortable with and has used before. Depending upon the movement of these decision makers in the insurance industry, a lawyer can gain or lose a client overnight. I've been on the winning and losing end when insurance adjustors have changed jobs. The most devastating was the loss of my client Assure Medical.

I left my old firm over 10 years ago to join Hand Arendall Harrison Sale, my present firm. I left because I had no significant clients of my own. I was trying cases for MedMutual, the largest medical malpractice insurer in Alabama. MedMutual was not my client and never would be. When I switched firms, I was almost 40-years old and realized without having your own clients, you are at the mercy of lawyers in your firm to keep you busy with legal work. Controlling a book of business gives a lawyer power within the firm.

I joined my new firm with no clients but with the goal to build the firm's basically non-existent medical malpractice business. I worked hard at developing new business and developed client relationships with Professional Risk, The Doctors Company, and Assure Medical, among others. Assure Medical was my largest client. I handled 20 - 25 cases for Assure Medical during a five-year span. I had a great relationship with one of the claims adjuster who selected Alabama counsel to defend Assure Medical's insured physicians. He began sending me cases in the northern part of Alabama even though Assure Medical had lawyers in northern Alabama to defend its doctors.

One day I received an email from the adjuster notifying me he would no longer be handling Alabama but would be transitioning to handling claims in Georgia and Florida. He told me a new person would be handling Alabama claims. The new Assure Medical claims guy used to work for MedMutual. I worked with him when I was with my former firm. I was told MedMutual fired him. Unfortunately, his landing spot was Assure Medical. Once I learned he would be handling Alabama claims, I knew my days of defending Assure Medical insured physicians were numbered. He took the Alabama work back to my old firm where he had a very good relationship with my old mentor Norman. It didn't matter how good of a job I did in defending Assure Medical's insured physicians. Assure Medical stopped sending me cases just as I expected. I did receive a nice email from the old adjuster complimenting me on my work:

"This is my last case in Alabama and I do want to let you know how much I enjoyed working with you on the several cases we worked on together. You are top shelf in my book and perhaps our paths will cross again. I started handling south Florida in September and I have been up to my eyeballs putting out fires. Great job on this case and all of the others you have handled for me."

It is incredibly frustrating to not have enough legal work at times to stay as busy as I would like. My compensation, which is related to my ownership interest in the firm, is based on performance. Performance is judged on originating legal fees through your own clients and the revenue brought in from my billable hours. As these performance measures decrease, my ownership interest and pay will necessarily decrease. And that's fair. I understand the pressures many people are under who are the sole providers for their family and face tough career changes. During the financial crisis, several of my friends and acquaintances who were the sole providers for their families lost their jobs and couldn't find another one. Although I have never lost a job, I understand the feelings of concern, nervousness and fear when your career is not going in the direction you had hoped, while at the same time, your family is relying upon you to be the provider. Past successes in the courtroom, academic success in college and graduate school, and past success in making money are all great. However, those past successes don't put food on the table and or pay college tuitions.

CHAPTER TWENTY-THREE
MY FAVORITE DENTIST CASE: A FEEL GOOD STORY

Shortly after Assure Medical took its work from me, I was assigned a case by a different Assure Medical adjuster to represent a local dentist. Apparently, Assure Medical assigned dental cases in Alabama through one adjuster and physician cases through another. Fortunately for me, the right hand didn't know what the left hand was doing. Had the Assure Medical claims guy who fired me known about the case, I'm sure he would have tried to send it to Norman.

This case was a tough one. The plaintiff, Cindy Jackson, went to see my client for a full-mouth reconstruction. Ms. Jackson had all of her teeth crowned 15 years before she saw my client. Her crowns were chipped, her bite was off, and she was having some pain in her jaw joints. My client evaluated Ms. Jackson and said he could give her new crowns. He charged Ms. Jackson $30,000 and required upfront payment.

There must be enough tooth structure in order for a tooth to support a crown. This is called a "ferrule." It was unclear whether some of Ms. Jackson's lower anterior teeth had enough tooth structure to hold crowns. Before placing permanent crowns, a dentist makes temporary crowns which are made of hard plastic. The dentist will use temporary cement and allow the patient to wear the temporary crowns to make sure they function appropriately and look good before placing the final crowns. The temporary crowns placed on Ms. Jackson came off pretty regularly. It is not uncommon for temporary crowns to come off the teeth supporting them. However, before placing permanent crowns, a dentist typically wants to see stability with the temporaries. After Ms. Jackson was in temporary crowns for 3-4 months, the dentist had her return to his office to install permanent crowns.

In the interim, Ms. Jackson had broken her top upper teeth to the gum line. These were the teeth that were going to anchor the upper crowns. My client was concerned he did not have enough tooth structure to hold the upper crowns in place. He moved forward with his treatment by placing posts and building up what remained of the upper teeth. His original plan was for individual crowns on the upper teeth. Because he needed more support for the crowns, he changed the treatment plan to two upper bridges that met between Ms. Jackson's two front teeth.

After several more months of treatment, the dentist installed permanent crowns, both upper and lower. Ms. Jackson immediately began having problems with the crowns. A very large gap was evident between the two front teeth, and the permanent bottom crowns would not stay on. The relationship between my client and Ms. Jackson deteriorated. At her final visit, both were basically yelling at the other. Ms. Jackson stormed out after my client dismissed her as a patient. My client did not return the $30,000 Ms. Jackson had paid for her crowns.

Ms. Jackson sued my client for dental malpractice. After a year and a half of litigation, including depositions and expert witness retention and discovery, the case went to trial. This was going to be a tough case. On the surface, what happened looked pretty bad for my dentist. He took Ms. Jackson's $30,000 for a new full-mouth reconstruction with crowns, and at the end of the treatment, her mouth was in no better shape than it was with the old crowns. For a dental case, this case was extremely complex and involved temporomandibular joint dysfunction issues, anterior guidance, crown lengthening surgery, whether implants should have been used, and various other dental issues. Basically, this case involved every dental issue you could imagine.

Getting the right jury was going to be crucial. I needed to find jurors who would not make up their mind before hearing our case and were analytical, a tall order for a Mobile County jury. At trial, I intended to methodically go through each visit Ms. Jackson had with my client and his treatment during each visit. I knew Ms. Jackson's lawyers would try the case by showing her mouth was in worse shape than it was before my client's treatment and we kept her money anyway. They would stay away from the details of the treatment and why my client did what he did – both of which were the strengths of our case.

Jury selection is always interesting. It is anything but exact science. The term "jury selection" is really a misnomer. The lawyers for each side do not select a jury - they strike the jurors they don't want and who's left compromises the jury. For example, assuming there is a jury panel of 36 potential jurors, 14 jurors out of the 36 will be selected, two of which are alternates. So, 22 potential jurors out of the panel must be eliminated or struck. That means each side has 11 strikes. The last strike by each side are the alternates. Alternates go through the entire trial process and, if are not needed, are dismissed prior to jury deliberations.

So during the *voir dire* process, the time for questioning potential jurors, the lawyers on both sides seek to find jurors who they do not want and will strike those jurors after *voir dire* has ended. Plaintiff's lawyers will strike jurors who are the most intelligent, affluent, and well-educated, including those who are professionals. Doctors, accountants, and architects rarely find their way on to a jury in a civil case. Defense lawyers typically want to strike the least intelligent, uneducated, and liberal potential jurors. Ms. Jackson's counsel did not strike a juror who worked in medical billing for a local physician group. That person turned out to be the foreman of the jury and was apparently very influential in the deliberation process.

The case tried for a week. As expected, Ms. Jackson's counsel tried the case on a very broad, overarching theme, basically arguing a dentist should "do no harm." They argued my client's treatment of Ms. Jackson harmed her because she left his office in worse shape than when she began, and he kept all of her $30,000. We tried the case by painstakingly going through each of Ms. Jackson's treatment visits and having my client explain what he did on each visit and why he did it. I had my client come down from the witness stand and draw various diagrams to explain important dental concepts. We used a skull with a movable jaw to demonstrate what TMJ was. My client had taken x-rays and did a CT scan of Ms. Jackson that he was able to manipulate from the witness stand. The computer program my client used for his CTs actually contained a picture of Ms. Jackson's skull, including her jaw and teeth, that could be rotated 360 degrees. My client impressively manipulated the CT scans from the witness stand with the laptop we provided to him as he interpreted the CT scan for the jury.

In defending a healthcare provider, you want to show the jury the provider has the three C's - Competence, Credibility, and Caring. The caring part of the case was a little difficult because my client and Ms. Jackson became combative toward each other near the end of the treatment. However, my client testified he was sorry about the relationship deteriorating and had it not become so bad, he would have continued working on Ms. Jackson. With regard to competence and credibility, having my client teach the jury the dental concepts in the case (especially by having him come off the witness stand and use charts, visual aids, and the CT scan) emphasized his competency and credibility.

As happens in most of my cases, I became very close to my client. Throughout the trial process, I realized what an exceptional dentist and how smart my client is. I told him from the beginning this was not going to be an easy case to win. However, we both agreed his care and treatment of Ms. Jackson did not breach the standard of care. We met for hours upon hours in preparing him for trial. He performed extremely well on direct examination and handled some curve balls on cross very well too. After an exhausting five days of trial, the jury returned a defense verdict in my client's favor. Ms. Jackson's lawyers were visibly shocked at the verdict. They believed they had a slam dunk case.

The verdict was incredibly rewarding for both my client and me. The trial gave my client vindication for his care and treatment, which had been so severely criticized. He had been practicing for over 30 years, was considering winding down his practice, and did not want to go out with a jury finding that he breached the standard of care in treating a patient. I needed the result for my professional psyche. My prior trial was the *Luna* case where we got popped for such a large verdict. In *Luna,* though, I was surrounded by co-defendants and their lawyers pointing the finger at my client. The *Jackson* case was one-on-one - Ms. Jackson's lawyers against me. What was also so great about the verdict was my client was an Assure Medical insured. I'm pretty sure this case was the first Assure Medical case tried to verdict in Alabama.

The Assure Medical claims' guy who took the physician cases away from me apparently caught wind of the case going to trial and emailed me on the second day of trial asking about the status of the case. I had no communication whatsoever with him at any time during the pendency of the case, and here he was on the second day of trial asking me about the case. I have absolutely no doubt in my mind that he was hoping I would lose the case so he could tell his bosses that if my old firm had been handling the case, they would have won. After the trial, my client sent to me an email praising my efforts and copied the Assure Medical adjuster who hired me on the case. The following is a portion of this email:

"Rod, I again want to thank you for all your efforts on my behalf over the past two years. Yesterday's verdict was a victory for both of us. Your representation of my case has been stellar and was handled and presented throughout the entire process with a level of class and dignity that has elicited an unprecedented level of pride, assurance and confidence for all in the fairness and justice of our legal system. Your approach was in stark contrast with that of the plaintiff and I am certain was most obvious to the jury as they were interested only in hearing the truth and evidence in our case rather than the theatrics and ridicule presented by the plaintiff's attorney.

I am most grateful as I feel I have not only gained the vindication I was seeking but I have also gained a relationship of trust and respect for you as my future attorney and my trusted friend. Rod, I will be forever grateful to you and your firm for your belief, support and representation of me throughout this difficult endeavor."

After receiving that email, Assure Medical's adjuster emailed my client to let him know that someone from Assure Medical's marketing department wanted to contact him to interview him about the case to use it in their marketing materials. In replying to this email, my client wrote:

"The excellent support and belief in my innocence which I witnessed from Rod Cate … continued to give me the willingness, confidence and resolve to persist regardless of the inconveniences and time experienced in the preparation process. I was convinced of my innocence and could not yield without seeking justice to its conclusion. I must sincerely say, that I never lost faith that vindication was possible as Mr. Cate's persistence, organization and thoroughness was apparent throughout the entire process, but it really wasn't until experiencing it firsthand at trial, that I saw true professionalism, legal genius and expertise at work on my behalf." (I know what you're thinking, but I promise you, I didn't write this, my client did.)

I don't know how Assure Medical used this case and my client's comments for its marketing materials, as the lawyer who my client so heavily praised (me), is the lawyer Assure Medical fired.

CHAPTER TWENTY-FOUR
NOTHING IS CERTAIN

At the time I am writing this, I am 52 years old. I've begun to take an inventory of my life, thinking about the decisions I've made in the past, decisions I need to make now, and what the rest of my life will look like. I guess this is sort of like a mid-life crisis with no crisis. It's hard to imagine in less than 20 years I'll be 70 years-old. I realize 70 now is not like being 70 fifty years ago. Turning 70 fifty years ago was knocking on death's door. Being 70 now, or 20 years from now, while being old, is not the beginning of the death march. Oddly enough, with my physical limitations and the body aches that come with aging, especially for me - lower back, hip, and ankle joint twinges of pain from the way I walk - I still feel like I'm 30 years old.

My biggest fear is going through a rapid deterioration in my condition. I do not want to be 60 years old and walking with a walker (with the tennis balls on the legs) or riding on a scooter just to get somewhere. I have noticed over the past three to five years a deterioration in my condition. Walking has become much more difficult than it was even ten years ago. And because walking has become more difficult, I walk less. Whether significant deterioration happens by 60, 65, or 70, the reality is the time left to enjoy somewhat normal physical activities is limited. My neurologist explained that as we all age, we have fewer and fewer cells. We all deteriorate. My deterioration will be more pronounced. That's why I exercise every day. I'm afraid of deteriorating.

So, sitting here at 52 with a job that has been fantastic in the past, but lately has been slower, a marriage that is pretty solid, and kids that are, for the most part grown, what is the next step? The brain is an amazing thing. At least for me, and I would assume for most people, the brain will not allow me to focus on my mortality. Sure, there are times I think about death and how things would be with my family if I were no longer here. If everyone constantly focused on their death, I think people would make different decisions about their life, especially when they reach middle age. Knowing that the amount of time left on this Earth is becoming less and less, you would think people would focus more on doing things to make them happy the rest of their lives instead of continuing the daily grind and dealing with the minutia and issues of daily life. I guess some people reach a certain age and just say "screw it," and make radical, life changing decisions to pursue a more enjoyable life while they can still do it.

I think a lot depends on a person's financial situation. I know if I had enough money today where I could call it quits, get my kids through college, and be able to pay my bills, I would do it in a second. Unfortunately, I'm nowhere near that position. I have worked with lawyers who were in their upper 70s and mid-80s. Their practices had slowed to basically nothing. They had an office and secretarial support, but little work. And, they came to work every day. They had plenty of money and could have traveled the world if they had wanted. They didn't. I think it is because that generation of lawyers felt they were defined by their careers. They were lawyers and couldn't imagine not being one.

At some point, I believe most people come to the realization that they will not accomplish many of the goals they've set. Of course, the best way not to disappoint yourself in not reaching your goals is not to set any. I'm somewhat kidding here. I've never really set goals in my life that I've wanted to meet by a certain date. I might have been in better shape, at least financially, at this point had I done so. But again, my thought on the key to happiness and the key to believing you have led a successful life is to revel in the small successes and experiences in your life. Up to this point in my life, I would consider myself to be a success with career happiness, family happiness, and incredible happiness with my network of close friends. I would not consider my life at this point to be successful financially. I am presently comfortable but no means wealthy, and the frightening part is there are no guarantees as to financial success from this day forward.

CHAPTER TWENTY-FIVE
THE DUNNAM TRIAL

The most rewarding case I ever tried was the *Dunnam* case. I tried it in the Mobile County Circuit Court in the early 2000s. I was brought in late to try the case after several years of the case bouncing back and forth to the Alabama Supreme Court on pre-trial issues. I represented two psychiatrists who were in their final year of residency at the University of South Alabama in Mobile. My clients were Dr. O. and Dr. M. (although public record, out of respect for their privacy, I do not disclose the names of my physician clients). Dr. O. was from Nigeria and Dr. M. was from Egypt. The case tried shortly after 9/11, and I was a little worried the South Alabama jury would be biased against my clients, since they were foreigners. Although both African, Egypt is close enough to the Middle East that a Mobile jury wouldn't appreciate the distinction. I developed an extremely close relationship with my clients, probably more so than any clients I represented - even up to now. They were both incredibly scared, nervous, and unfamiliar with the American judicial system. They had just started their practices as psychiatrists and certainly did not want a verdict against them. This was the first medical case I tried as "first chair." This means I didn't have the safety net of my mentor Norman.

The allegations against Dr. O. and Dr. M. were that they were treating a patient who was involuntarily committed to a psychiatric hospital and breached the standard of care by discharging the patient, who committed suicide eight days later. Making the case somewhat difficult to try was that the patient's medical chart contained several notations quoting him stating he was *"going to blow his brains out with his father's shotgun"* when he got out of the facility. Unfortunately, that's exactly what happened. Making the trial of the case even more difficult was that the judge (the same one who asked me if I had a problem standing when addressing the court) allowed the jury to see photographs taken at the scene showing the dead patient's head following the shotgun blast. They showed blood splattered all over the walls of his house. These photos had no relevance to the case. Both sides stipulated that the decedent shot himself in the head. There was absolutely no evidentiary purpose for allowing these photos in to evidence. The only purpose for letting the jury see the pictures was to attempt to invoke sympathy and emotion in the jurors' decision. The jury simply did not need to see the gruesome pictures.

The trial was not particularly long. It started on a Monday. The jury reached a verdict by that Friday. But like all trials, I tried the case during the day, spoke with my clients for an hour or so after the trial to give an assessment of how the day went, and then went back to the office to work late into the evening to prepare for the next day. Adding to the difficulty of the trial was that Dr. O. spoke with a thick Nigerian accent and was very hard to understand. Dr. M. was extremely soft spoken and had an Egyptian accent. Despite these issues, they both testified incredibly well and were able to effectively explain to the jury their decision making process in discharging the patient.

Closing arguments started after lunch on the Thursday of trial. My preference is to conclude the evidence at the end of one day and have a night to prepare for closings. It was a lot more difficult to give a closing argument beginning in an afternoon when I had spent the first part of the day examining and cross-examining witnesses. The closing went well. I don't think I have ever been as emotionally invested in a case. I wanted to win the case so badly for my clients. My emotion spilled into my close. I went after the patient's lawyer hard for some of the unsupported allegations he made. I passionately defended my clients' treatment. I passionately defended that my clients were from Africa. During my close, I thought to myself I might be too emotional. Typically, plaintiff lawyers use emotion to their benefit during closing arguments. Defense lawyers are more methodical and focus on the evidence and testimony – basically trying to undo the emotion created by plaintiffs' lawyers.

I never let off the gas in my closing. I remained highly emotional throughout closing. What I was saying felt good coming out, and I kept going with it. I love giving closing arguments. It is so much fun "being in the zone" where all your thoughts crystallize and you feel this command over every word you speak. The physical exhaustion from the three-week trial preparation and the week-long trial itself along with my intense desire to win the case so badly for my clients, left me emotionally drained when I finished my closing argument. I was so emotionally, mentally, and physically exhausted that tears welled up in my eyes when I sat back down. I recall barely listening to the plaintiff's lawyers' rebuttal closing argument.

The judge gave the jury their instructions. The jury began deliberating at around 3:00 p.m. Waiting for a jury to come back with a verdict is in itself cruel and unusual punishment. Once the jury leaves the jury box and retires to the jury room to begin deliberating, we begin packing up the file, visual aids, and the audiovisual machines, but always listening for the knock on the jury room door signifying the jury has reached a verdict. It is impossible to know what the jury's decision is until they actually read it. However, in my experience, if the jury returns a verdict fairly quickly (within one to one and a half hours or less), I always feel pretty good. A quick decision is typically for the defendant since it usually takes longer for a jury to find for a plaintiff and then arrive at an amount of damages.

… 3:30 p.m., no verdict, 4:30 p.m., no verdict. At 5:00 p.m., the judge reentered the courtroom to check on the jury's progress. No decision yet, and no decision was imminent. The judge sent the jury home for the night and instructed everyone to reconvene at 9:00 the next morning. Not a good feeling. I scrutinized each juror's demeanor as they walked out of the courtroom that night but wasn't really able to get a read on any of them. They all stared blankly into space and made no eye contact with anyone on the plaintiff or defense side. I went home, tried to relax, and watch a little TV. I did not eat much dinner. By Thursday night of trial week, I had eaten so little during the week that I wasn't particularly hungry. I lost five pounds during that week, as was typical for any trial. While watching TV, I saw a story on the scroll at the bottom of the screen on one of the news channels where a New York jury returned a $6 million verdict against a psychiatric hospital that had discharged a mental patient who had killed himself by leaping off of the hospital's parking deck. At first I thought I had just imagined this until the story scrolled across the bottom of the screen again five minutes later. I hoped that none of the jurors home watching TV had seen the story.

After a couple of hours of sleep, I returned to the courtroom the next morning to greet my incredibly nervous clients. I did the best I could to comfort them. The waiting began again as the jury started deliberations at 9:00 a.m. In an Alabama civil case, the law requires a unanimous agreement by all 12 jurors to find for either the plaintiff or the defendant. If all 12 jurors cannot agree, a mistrial results, and the case get tried all over again at a later date.

In other trials I've had, some of the plaintiff lawyers station a staff member close to the jury room door to try to listen to the deliberations. Certain firms are notorious for doing this. If a plaintiff's lawyer from one of these firms attempted to settle the case while the jury was deliberating, it meant the staff member could hear the deliberations and they were not good for the plaintiff's case. Certain lawyers, upon hearing this information, would try to get some money out of the case before the jury came back with its verdict. This was not the case in the *Dunnam* trial.

At 10:30 a.m. there was a loud knock on the jury room door. The judge came out, and the lawyers and parties took their positions at counsel table. Everyone stood as the jury returned to the jury box. I told my clients as I typically did, *"No matter the result, show no emotion or reaction one way or the other until the jury is dismissed."* The judge then asked the foreman of the jury if they had reached a verdict. The foreman replied that they had. I was especially nervous at this point because the foreman of the jury was a gentleman on the front row who, based upon his body language and facial expressions, seemed to be leaning toward the plaintiff. The judge asked the foreman to read the verdict. The two seconds from the end of the judge's statement until the foreman spoke seemed to take forever:

"WE THE JURY FIND IN FAVOR OF THE DEFENDANTS AND AGAINST THE PLAINTIFF."

Tears streamed down Dr. O.'s and Dr. M.'s faces. The case had been litigated for over two years, and my clients could not contain their relief. I fought back tears myself just watching them. The judge then polled the jury, asking each juror individually if the verdict read aloud was their verdict. All answered affirmatively, and the judge dismissed the jury. At that point, my clients hugged me and couldn't stop thanking me for everything I had done. I walked up to the judge's clerk to tend to some administrative matters and had a quick conversation with the judge and the plaintiff's lawyer. When I walked out of the courtroom into the hallway, I saw a scene that I will never forget to this day. The jurors were all around my clients hugging them and crying tears of joy with them! The jurors began coming up to me to shake my hand telling me what a great job I had done. Again, I had to fight back the tears. I realized that moment would never be topped during the rest of my legal career. No trial has come close to the professional satisfaction from trying that case.

CHAPTER TWENTY-SIX
MY TRIP TO INDIA

One of the most rewarding aspects of the *Luna* case was that I had to travel to India. Luna's counsel insisted on viewing and videotaping the facilities where the transcription of the discharge summary took place. It was first transcribed and reviewed by transcriptionists at Trantech, InTran's subcontractor, and then reviewed for a final time by InTran. We also scheduled the depositions of InTran's corporate representatives and transcriptionist. InTran was based in Mumbai (formerly known as Bombay). Trantech was located in Noida.

We made the trip in August. I thought Mobile was hot and steamy in August. Mumbai was on a different level of hot and humid. The flight to Mumbai left from JFK airport in New York at 8 p.m. The flights from Mobile to JFK were terrible. I had to leave Mobile on a 6 a.m. flight to Houston and sat through a 4- hour layover in Houston before flying to JFK. I had another 5 hours to wait at JFK before the flight left to Mumbai. I'd been traveling for 15 hours before my 16-hour flight from JFK for Mumbai.

Sixteen hours on a plane is a long time. I slept, watched 3 movies, and had 2 meals. Stir crazy doesn't come close to describing it. Thank goodness my client hooked me up with a first class seat. My seat laid completely flat. I'm 6'2" and could stretch out all the way. I basically had my own compartment with a TV. I was given a box containing various items for comfort. My favorite thing was a pair of thick socks to put on to wear instead of shoes. I couldn't imagine flying coach for 16 hours. I'll have to admit I felt like a pretty big deal sitting up front.

I land in Mumbai. It's around 11 p.m. Time is completely flip-flopped. Six p.m. in Mumbai is 6 a.m. in Mobile. Actually, there is another 30-minute difference in there for some reason. So, when I arrive, even though my body is telling me it's morning and time to get up, it's nighttime and time to go to bed again. The time difference and the excitement of being in a different country would not let me sleep. I lied in bed all night wide awake. By the time I felt sleepy, it was time to get up to go to InTran's corporate office to prepare its employees for depositions. I worked on adrenaline that day. I was so tired and remember how I just wanted to go to sleep.

I stayed at the Oberoi Hotel in Mumbai. It was a true 5-star hotel. No cars could pull up to the hotel without going through a gate and bomb check by armed guards. Entering the hotel was like going through security at the airport. Once inside, the place was incredible. Beautiful Indian women worked the check-in counter, which wasn't a counter but actually several individual desks facing chairs where you sit while checking in. The lobby was huge and made of white marble with a black marble statue and red piano in the middle. It was open to the top of the hotel. The ceiling was made of skylights. The rooms had great ocean views. What made the Oberoi really stand out was the service. I couldn't walk 10 steps without someone asking me if I needed anything.

One thing that sticks in my mind about India is the hospitality and service shown by everyone. During the two long days of deposition preparation, someone was always bringing me food and drinks. Bottled water was a necessity. I was told to keep my mouth closed in the shower to make sure I didn't swallow any water. I used bottled water to brush my teeth.

Another thing that stood out about Mumbai was how crowded the city was. Mumbai is the ninth most populous city in the world with a population of over 18 million. It was only about 10 miles from the Oberoi to InTran's offices, but the trip took a couple of hours depending on the time of day. The streets are jammed with what look like 1950s style miniature taxis, known as Padminis. They are all painted black and yellow. The honking is incessant. As opposed to taxi drivers in Manhattan who rudely honk to get someone to move or get out of their way, the honking in Mumbai is just to let the other drivers know there is a taxi coming up on them.

InTran's CFO Samar Jindal picked me up each morning. I enjoyed taking in what I could see of Indian culture on my way to work each morning. Weddings are big in India. I saw huge banners with pictures of the bride and groom seemingly advertising weddings. These banners stretched between thin poles about 30 feet high. They were everywhere. One thing that caught my attention was the number of motorcycles weaving in and out of traffic. It was common to see an entire family riding on a motorcycle. I regularly saw a husband and wife with a couple of kids riding on what looked like an American-type dirt bike motorcycle. I even saw a mother riding on the back of a motorcycle sitting sidesaddle and holding her infant.

I also saw a lot of begging and poverty. India is a poor country. There is a vast difference between the haves and the have-nots. InTran's CEO told me anyone with an education and the desire to work hard can do well in India. It was obvious how much growth was taking place in Mumbai. New construction was everywhere. Yet, I still saw cows in the roads and on the sidewalks.

After the first day of deposition preparation, we went out to dinner at the Taj Hotel for an authentic Indian meal. I was dragging from lack of sleep. The meal consisted of what seemed to be various pureed meats with potatoes, rice, and sauces. You take what looks like a piece of pita bread and scoop up the different foods and pop it in your mouth. All done with your hands. The meal was delicious. I paid for it the next day and for several days later. It was tough having to go to the bathroom constantly while trying to get witnesses ready for deposition. That, plus my body clock not adjusting, made for a rough few days. The depositions went okay. I had to work a lot with my witnesses on how to answer questions without volunteering unnecessary, potentially damaging information. There was a big cultural difference between American and Indian witnesses in that the Indian witnesses' nature is to be more forth coming and helpful. A great human quality overall, but not so good when giving a deposition.

The day after the InTran depositions concluded, I flew to New Delhi for video inspection of Trantech's facility and the depositions of Trantech's transcriptionists and company representative. My flight was not until the afternoon. That morning, Samar picked me up and gave me a great tour of Mumbai. Mumbai is the capital of India and has some beautiful buildings. Of course, there is a lot of British architecture. The most architecturally stunning building I have ever seen in my life is the Chhatrapati Shivaji Terminus in Mumbai. It is a train station built in 1888. I'm not an architectural expert, but I do know the building had some Gothic style. It is about 5-6 stories high and has pointed arches, turrets and a statue on top of the tallest dome roof in the middle of the building. I loved the large working clock directly below the statue. I've included a photo of it.

Samar and I had lunch at the cricket club in Mumbai. We sat in an open air dining room watching cricket players practice. It was a pretty cool lunch. Samar dropped me off at the airport for my flight to New Delhi and for depositions I knew were not going to take place. The Trantech facility where the transcription in the *Luna* case was first transcribed was located in Noida, India, which was about 20 miles southeast of New Delhi. Prior to making the trip to India, Luna's counsel enlisted Indian lawyers from New Delhi to obtain an order requiring Trantech's depositions and inspection of the facility in Noida. Luna's counsel had a suspicion Trantech's witnesses might not show up. Trantech decided it would not defend itself in the *Luna* case and just take its chances, realizing any judgment against it would be difficult to collect in India.

While I was still in Mumbai, the CEO of Trantech traveled to Mumbai to meet with us to discuss his deposition. Trantech's CEO told us he was not going to sit for a deposition even though there was a court order requiring him to do so. We had no control over him. We suggested it was in our interest for him to go forward with his deposition, but he refused.

InTran arranged for me to have a driver at my disposal while in New Delhi. He drove me from New Delhi to Noida for the Trantech depositions and inspection even though I knew the depositions were not going forward. When we arrived at the Trantech facility, I was shocked at how horrible the outside of the facility appeared. InTran's facility was state of the art and housed in a new high rise. In contrast, Trantech was located in the industrial section of Noida, which is broken down into sectors. The sector in which Trantech was located contained dilapidated buildings on dirt streets surrounded by chain link fences with barbed wire.

Once all the lawyers arrived, we attempted to enter the Trantech compound but were refused entry. Luna's counsel and their local Indian counsel telephoned the judge who issued the order requiring the depositions to go forward to let him know about Trantech's refusal to allow entry to its facility. Fifteen minutes later, the judge arrived at the Trantech facility. The judge, Luna's counsel and Indian counsel, and a person who represented himself as the brother of Trantech's CEO went inside the facility for a meeting. Thirty minutes later, all of the parties came out of Trantech. We were told the depositions and inspection of the facility would not take place. From the little I saw of India's judicial system, it appeared somewhat corrupt. To this day, I have no idea what happened in Noida that morning and why we were refused access to Trantech. I suspect someone from Trantech had some influence over the judge or even paid him off so that no depositions or inspection would go forward.

The court reporter and videographer were present in Noida that morning waiting with the rest of us outside of the Trantech. The temperature was around 95 degrees Fahrenheit. Everyone was sweating. There was also an uneasy feeling among the lawyers standing outside. We were clearly out of place, and the local residents were suspiciously watching us. After Luna's counsel came out of the facility, he made a statement transcribed by the court reporter and filmed by the videographer explaining how he had obtained the proper court order to go forward with the depositions and inspection of Trantech, that he was prohibited from entering Trantech's facility, and the Trantech deponents who were required to appear for deposition failed to appear. The other lawyers representing co-defendants in the case made statements on the record, and I also made a statement on the video just noting my appearance at the site.

One of the worst evidentiary rulings I've ever seen in my life occurred during the *Luna* trial when the judge allowed Luna's counsel to play to the jury his self-serving video statement in front of the Trantech facility. The judge overruled our objections even though playing the statement was clearly inadmissible. Lawyers cannot testify at trial. Allowing Luna's counsel to play his video statement was no different than allowing him to take the stand at trial testifying to what had happened.

The day after the trip to Noida, I met with Trantech's counsel in New Delhi. I was at my hotel and received a call from Trantech's counsel requesting a meeting that day. I had no idea what to expect but had my driver take me to the offices of Trantech's lawyers. Once I got there, I was led into a conference room where there were at least three lawyers present, as well as the person who was present at Trantech the day before who had identified himself as the brother of Trantech's CEO. Because Trantech was a subcontractor of InTran, Trantech and their lawyers were very deferential to me.

Before the meeting began, another lawyer, who was apparently the managing partner for the firm, came into the room to ask about what had happened the day before. We discussed those events. Then the lawyer told me they were considering bringing a foreign corrupt practices act case against Luna's counsel and his firm based on the method in which they obtained the order from the Indian judge requiring Trantech to appear for depositions and allow inspection of its facility. There was a suggestion of a pay-off to the judge for the order. I had no response to that and didn't really care. But what came next left my head spinning. I was told that consideration had been given to *"making Luna's counsel disappear."* I was told people go missing from the Noida area all the time, and it would not have been difficult to make Luna's counsel "disappear." It may have been just a joke, and I didn't pick up on it. Regardless, I walked out of the meeting thinking how glad

I was that my flight back home was in a couple of days.

I had a free day before my flight back home so I decided to go see the Taj Mahal. I had access to a private driver and figured this would be my one and only trip to India in my life so why not go see one of the seven wonders of the world. (The Taj Mahal is not one of the original seven wonders of the world. The original seven wonders are all from ancient Greece. The Taj Mahal is actually one of the "new" seven wonders, along with the pyramids of Egypt, the Great Wall of China, Stonehenge, etc.) The Taj Mahal is located in Agra, a 4-hour drive from New Delhi. We left at 6 a.m. and started the journey. The drive gave me the opportunity to see the Indian countryside. Where we were was very arid and hot, desert-like. We passed some beautiful temples along the way. We had to stop when we crossed into a new state so the driver could pay some tariff. The driver had to go inside a building and left me in the car with it running, windows up and doors locked. He told me under no circumstances was I to roll the windows down or unlock the doors. As soon as he was out of sight, several people came up to the car and began tapping on the window trying to sell me Indian trinkets. One guy had a monkey on his arm that was turning back flips and doing other tricks. It was an uncomfortable 15 minutes as I tried to ignore this circus going on outside the car. Finally, my driver returned and shooed everyone away, and we continued our trip.

I had no knowledge of the Taj Mahal's history. The Taj Mahal is a mausoleum built in the mid-1600s at the request of an emperor to house the tomb of his favorite wife. We've all seen pictures of the Taj Mahal, so I won't describe it here other than to say seeing it in person blew me away. It is constructed of white marble. When you enter the grounds, you have this grand view of the tomb (the big white building in the pictures). There is a reflecting pond lined with sculpted trees that reflects the image of the tomb on the water. It is a stunning view. What you don't see from pictures is the intricate, inlaid semi-precious stone work on the marble walls of the tomb. The patterns and pictures of the semi-precious stones in the marble made me shake my head in amazement. It was beautiful.

Of course, I got a great picture of me in front of the tomb. It's framed and on my wall in my TV room upstairs. I occasionally look at it and think how lucky I was to be able to make the India trip. Some big time lawyers in the large big-city firms travel all over the world for work, but not me. This trip was special. I was lucky to get the *Luna* case, lucky that Luna's lawyer insisted on going to India, and lucky to have had one of the greatest experiences of my life.

CHAPTER TWENTY-SEVEN
MY CHILDHOOD AND THE CYC

The long flight back from India gave me time to reflect on how far I had come from the night I broke my neck and all the great things I've been able to accomplish and experience even going through life as a handi. I wasn't patting myself on the back, but was just putting in to perspective how my life had turned out to that point. I thought a lot about my childhood and how incredible it was that someone who grew up primarily in small, country towns and had such a basic, simple childhood could have just finished a 10-day stint working as a lawyer in India.

I guess any story autobiographical in nature is not complete without some view in to the author's childhood. The dilemma is - a cursory look into the author's childhood is meaningless whereas an exhaustive look becomes boring and monotonous. How a child is raised – family dynamics, expectations, love, nurturing, experiences, etc. – is the most determinative aspect of the kind of adult a child becomes. And yes, I'm stating the obvious. But the unfair part of this is none of us had any control over whether we had great, average, or terrible childhoods. So, how we view the world, how we react to life, what kind of person we will be – basically our fundamental building blocks - are predominately shaped outside of our control.

Based on how we were raised, we can have different ways of viewing the same thing. The fact that people don't think just like you or react to a situation just like you doesn't mean there's something wrong with them. My theory is people who were raised in similar fashions have basic similar views of the world. How many times have you thought or said, *"I can't believe how this guy is reacting."* Every person brings their own background in to how they deal with everyday situations. Just because I react a certain way about a situation doesn't mean I'm right. I may have it all wrong and can't understand the other person's view based upon my fundamental beliefs learned during childhood.

Similarly, our personalities are shaped by our childhoods. Were you poor? Were you affluent? Did your parents fight all the time? Were your parents divorced? Was a parent an alcoholic? Were your parents affectionate? Were you abused? It goes on and on. We all walk through a minefield from birth to adolescence. Fortunate are those that make it through without getting blown up.

I was one of the fortunate ones. I had a great childhood with supportive, caring, loving parents, who provided a stable, nurturing environment. I grew up with three sisters and a brother. Valerie and Lisa were the oldest, followed by my brother Mike, who was 14 months older than I. Libby was the youngest, two years behind me. At one point in the year, we are all nominally two years apart. My earliest recollection is being 4 years old and living in Roanoke, Virginia. My Dad was a sports writer for *The Roanoke Times*.

I have no recollection of ever being inside. All my memories are of playing outside from dawn until dusk. I spent hours playing in a nearby creek, catching crayfish and minnows, and making an aquarium out of an empty Charles Chip cookie tin. Back in the late 60s and early 70s, Charles Chip delivered potato chips and cookies in round, metal containers. I used to love seeing the Charles Chip truck pull up outside our house. We played football, wiffle-ball, and four square. We walked to the drug store where a quarter could buy a ton of candy. Games of "kick the can" lasted until it became so dark you couldn't see. We played outside all day until we heard my Mom ring the cow bell letting us know dinner was ready. It was just an idyllic young childhood.

We moved to Athens, Tennessee just before I started the third grade. My grandmother Emmagene lived in Athens. I had no idea why we moved to Athens, but something bad must have happened with my Dad's job at the newspaper. You don't move in with your Dad's mother unless you have to. We stayed in Athens two years. I loved it. Emmagene lived in a big house directly across the street from Ingleside Elementary School. My Dad attended Ingleside when he was a kid. I had the same principal that my Dad had. It was a comfortable feeling growing up in the same small town as your Dad. At this time, I first discovered I excelled in athletics and academics. Mike and I played all the little league sports and both did very well. We won everything and were the stars of our teams. School came easy to me. I had the same drive to be the best in the classroom as I did on the field or court. The first B I ever made in my life was a B+ in Calculus at Davidson.

Athens is the home of Mayfields Dairy. My great grandfather Bryant Mayfield started Mayfields. Emmagene's brothers Tom and Scott Mayfield ran Mayfields. At the time we lived in Athens (1974-1976), Emmagene, Tom, Scott and their sister Sallie each owned 25% of the company. Emmagene had a refrigerator/freezer in her garage that was filled twice a week by a Mayfields' delivery guy. Back then Mayfields made milk, ice cream, tea, lemonade, cottage cheese, and some other products. We had an endless supply. Emmagene was fairly wealthy, but we certainly didn't live like we were rich. Money was never something I even thought about. Again, all we did was play sports and play outside until dark. Skateboarding had come to the South and became our mode of transportation. I had long hair and we looked like a bunch of little hippies riding around in a pack on our skateboards.

At the end of each little league football season, the winners of each age division were rewarded with a trip to Huntsville, Alabama to tour the space center and play the corresponding age division champion from Huntsville. I went both years I lived in Athens. Huntsville was at least 10 times the size of Athens. Every year, the Athens' teams got the crap kicked out of them. Athens had a very small minority population. There may have been one or two black kids on my teams. Huntsville's teams were predominately black.

Getting your ass whipped by a clearly superior team was an eye opener. I even questioned maybe I was only good because I played against such poor competition – the big fish in the small pond.

My final Huntsville trip gave me some needed confidence. It was also a foreshadowing of what was coming next in my life. No Athens team ever stayed within 5 touchdowns of Huntsville. I remember warming up before the game and looking across the field to see the Huntsville team. They were all black and seemed so much larger than we were. I was sure another ass kick was on its way. We could do nothing on offense all day. We were just out-athleted. But we more then held our own on defense. We were losing 7-0 right before halftime. I was playing middle linebacker and was doing a pretty good job shutting down Huntsville. The Huntsville quarterback threw his first pass of the game, trying to surprise us. I intercepted the pass and ran 60 yards for a touchdown. We missed the 2-point conversion and went into halftime down 7-6. We lost the game 13-6, but really played this more talented Huntsville team tough.

The following year we moved to Emporia, Virginia and to a complete change in culture. My Dad had taken a job as the editor and publisher for the local weekly Emporia newspaper. Other than also being a small town, Emporia and Athens were nothing alike. Emporia was 60% black. Something I had never experienced before. Most of the affluent white families sent their kids to Brunswick Academy in the next county. My Dad would have never considered sending us to a private school. Emporia was still somewhat segregated. There were separate black and white youth sports leagues. On the surface, public schools were integrated. If I remember this correctly, and I think that I do, someone devised a scheme to pass students who just weren't quite ready to go to the next grade, a half grade. Half grades were predominately filled by black students and whole grades by whites. Even though 60% of the students were black, my sixth grade class was around 80% white. The fifth and a half grade was 95% black. That scheme was shut down eventually.

Youth sports' leagues were open to any race, but typically the black kids played in their leagues and the white kids in theirs. Some black kids ventured over to the white leagues for baseball, but that was about it. No white kids played in the black league. That is until the Cates rolled in to town. My brother and I played our first football season in Emporia in the white league. I was in the fifth grade, Mike in the sixth. The season went well. My Dad coached us our first year in Athens and wanted to coach our second year in Emporia. He was told, "no." Not caring for that response, Dad took Mike and I over to the Community Youth Center or the "CYC" - the black league - where Dad would coach and Mike and I play. There were 60 kids on the team, 58 black kids and the Cate brothers. Mike and I knew several of the players from school, so it wasn't as if we were going across town to play with kids we didn't know. But this was a big deal in town. White kids playing in the black league was unheard of.

There were no negative repercussions that I noticed. I was treated no differently by my friends or their families. The positive was I had a whole different group of teammates, who respected us for playing at the CYC. Our teammates were unaware the only reason we were playing at the CYC was that my Dad was not allowed to coach the white team. I played quarterback and Mike played running back. We were not given our starting

money. Actually, it's not called "picking" tobacco but "priming." The kind of tobacco that was grown in North Carolina ripens from the bottom up. So, to harvest the tobacco, you pick the leaves that are "prime" to harvest. This harvesting is different from Burley tobacco where the entire plant is cut all at once and cured. I'll never forget my first day in the tobacco fields. I had no idea what I was getting myself in to.

You show up just before dawn. The air is still a little cool and the tobacco plants are wet with dew. I was told to wear a long sleeve shirt, long pants, a water-proof jacket, shoes, and a baseball cap. Basically, make sure you are covered head to toe. Farmers sprayed the tobacco with chemicals that would make you sick if they soaked into your skin. You pick a row and you start with the first plant. It's first primings. You bend down and with a sweeping motion break the bottom several ripe leaves off the plant. You then slap the leaves under your weak hand armpit and repeat the process at the next plant. You keep going until you are carrying a huge bushel of tobacco leaves under your arm. You then walk over to the sled being pulled by a tractor and lay the leaves you picked on the sled. Then, head back to your next plant and keep working your way to the end of your row.

There was definitely a learning curve in being able to properly pick tobacco. The first time I did it, I probably cost the farmer money because I was so terrible. Breaking the leaves off where the stem meets the stalk of the plant and then slapping those leaves under your arm did take some skill. I didn't realize until I had finished picking leaves off my first 10 plants that all I was holding under my arm were broken-off stems. The brittle stems had broken away from the tobacco leaves either when I picked the leaves or when I was slapping the leaves under my arm to hold them until I had enough of a bushel. Talk about comical - tobacco leaves flying through the air with me holding only the broken stems. I got better.

Picking tobacco was the worst job I've ever done. Juice would shoot out of the plants when they were wet in the mornings and hit you in the eyes. The sting hurt so bad. You just kept going. Brown tobacco gum got caked all over your hands so you couldn't rub your eyes anyway. You reeked of tobacco. I always got sick after a day of picking from the chemicals. We made $3/hr. We'd typically take a mid-morning break and were treated to a pack of Nabs or an oatmeal pie and a Mountain Dew. I never worked in the tobacco barn hanging the tobacco leaves to cure. Five hours of picking was enough for me. I worked the tobacco fields for two summers. To me, it was a measure of toughness - a character builder. I'm glad I did it.

Summertime was not only tobacco picking season but also baseball season. I loved playing baseball and was good at it, but of the big three sports, it was third. I decided not to play summer baseball after my ninth grade year to focus on football at the high school level. Several of us went through "voluntary workouts" that summer. We worked primarily on defensive back drills. I remember being so tired at the end of a practice, I couldn't lift my arms to intercept a pass but just knocked it down with my helmet. I had never been in such great shape when football camp started. Little did I know it would all be over a week later.

CHAPTER TWENTY-NINE
THE COMPLETE BODY CASE: THE BEGINNING

Of all the cases I tried, the *Luna* case had the most disappointing result; the *Dunham* (suicide case) was the most rewarding; but the *Complete Body* case was just the best. Complete Body Formula was a dietary supplement. It came in a bottle with instructions to take one ounce per day mixed with juice, water, or some other liquid. Complete Body Formula contained every vitamin and mineral you could imagine. By the time this case started, Complete Body Formula had been on the market for 12 years and had a very devoted customer base. People of all ages used Complete Body Formula. However, elderly people consumed around 60% of all Complete Body Formula sold.

Larry Brown was the president/owner of Complete Body, Inc. Larry was nutrition conscious and used to take several vitamins in pill form. He had the idea to develop a liquid form of vitamin supplement where a person could take a one ounce shot of a liquid containing a wide array of vitamins and minerals, instead of swallowing multiple pills. Thus, the invention of Complete Body Formula.

Larry was not a chemist or food scientist and had no background or training as either. In doing some research, he found someone in Texas who knew enough to derive a formula of a dry powder mix containing multiple vitamin and minerals that could be diluted in liquid to develop what Larry envisioned. This person began manufacturing Complete Body Formula. Larry was very successful in selling Complete Body Formula. For the first 12 years of Complete Body Formula's existence, Larry had no problems with the product. He was making a good profit, and his customers gave him rave reviews.

Larry became well-acquainted with the person in charge of manufacturing Complete Body Formula. This person worked with the same company that had manufactured Complete Body Formula for the 12 years of its existence. He eventually switched jobs and started working for US Blending in Kansas. He convinced Larry to allow US Blending to manufacture Complete Body Formula. Larry knew very little about the manufacturing process and trusted this person since Complete Body Formula was made correctly for years.

Complete Body Formula was manufactured by using a formula that had the dry bulk amounts of vitamins and minerals that when blended with liquid, would contain the proper amounts per serving size. The problem was no one at US Blending seemed to have a clue as to the proper formula for Complete Body Formula. Someone at US Blending took a label from a bottle of Complete Body Formula and attempted to develop a new formula that would presumably result in the proper amounts of vitamins and minerals in a serving size.

The first problem that occurred was that the formula was wrong. The "new" formula did not take into consideration the conversion from the bulk amount of vitamins and minerals that were used when converting to the proper serving size when mixed with liquid. Another problem was that an employee of Southern Dry Mix, the company that was hired by US Blending to blend and manufacture the dry mix powder that went into the Complete Body Formula, apparently misread the formula and produced a dry mix with highly toxic amounts of selenium. Selenium is a dietary mineral that arguably has some health benefits. A one ounce serving of Complete Body Formula was supposed to contain 200 micrograms of selenium. The first production run for the dry powder mix for Complete Body Formula resulted in a dry mix that after blended with the liquid, contained 200 milligrams of selenium. The result of the manufacturing errors led to bottles of Complete Body Formula containing 1,000 times the amount of selenium they should have.

Larry Brown had no knowledge of this colossal screw-up. He was just the distributor of the product. Arguably, he could have taken a more active role to ensure the manufacturing process was done correctly, but Complete Body Formula had been manufactured with no problems for 12 years. Larry was not made aware of the fact that someone from US Blending actually had to attempt to reconfigure the formula based on a Complete Body Formula label. Tainted bottles of Complete Body Formula were shipped to Larry from Kansas to his office in Woodstock, Georgia. Larry placed the labels on the bottles and shipped them to retailers - mostly health food and drug stores.

About a month after Larry first received and shipped the bottles of Complete Body Formula that were for the first time manufactured at US Blending, Larry received a call from a drug store in Chipley, Florida notifying him that three of their customers who purchased and consumed Complete Body Formula were complaining about their hair falling out. It got worse. Before Larry could issue a recall, around 400 people, ages five years-old to 85 years old, who had consumed Complete Body Formula, were losing their hair and fingernails. Some had organ failure and various neuropathies. The lawsuits came quickly. One lawyer in the Florida panhandle filed a lawsuit representing 90 consumers of Complete Body Formula. Plaintiffs filed cases in Georgia, Tennessee, Alabama, Florida, North Carolina, South Carolina, and New York, both in federal and state courts. In the biz, we call this "mass tort litigation," a defense attorney's dream.

Zurich, the insurer of Complete Body, Inc., hired my firm to defend Complete Body in these cases. Because I had experience in mass tort litigation and class actions, the lawyer who had the Zurich work sent the case to me to handle. A lawyer never actually knows how big a case will eventually become when he first receives it. From the outset, this looked to be a major piece of litigation, and it was.

Larry Brown ran Complete Body out of a leased office/loading dock in a small industrial park in Woodstock, Georgia. Larry was in his early 60s and looked like Kenny Rogers, with silver hair and a beard. Larry was very religious and very personable. He felt horrible about what had happened. On top of feeling guilty for selling a product meant to help people that actually caused harm, Larry knew the business he started and grew for 12 years was dead.

Early in the case, I flew to Chicago to meet with lawyers for US Blending and Southern Dry Mix and all of the insurance adjusters. The purpose of the meeting was to attempt to work out an early resolution of the case and agree on a percentage of liability for each defendant. The meeting took place in October. The temperature was just beginning to become cool in Chicago, a welcome relief from the Mobile heat where the temperature was still in the 90s.

The lawyers for US Blending wanted to have a dinner meeting with me the night before the lawyer/adjuster conference the next morning. US Blending was represented by Pat Gloor and Don Ivansek from the Gloor Law Group. The Gloor Law Group was a Chicago firm of about 15 lawyers who had split from Cassiday Schade LLP, a large Chicago firm. The purpose of the dinner meeting was for the US Blending lawyers to attempt to establish an alliance with me where we would agree that Southern Dry Mix was primarily at fault. My early assessment of the case was that Southern Dry Mix should bear the lion's share of the liability because its improper reading of the formula appeared to me to be the most significant cause of the excess selenium.

I took an instant liking to Pat and Don. To this day, we are great friends. Pat was in his late-60s when I first met him. He is a great guy and is no-nonsense. Don is a little older than I am. He is a big guy of eastern European-Irish descent. Don is classic Chicago – grew up in Cicero. He is one of the most genuinely nice people I have ever met. The dinner was great and the drinks flowed. We agreed that Southern Dry Mix should absorb the greatest proportion of any agreed upon settlement. Pat picked up the tab. He always picked up the tab. The case lasted over three years. Depositions, meetings, and court hearings in Chicago, New Orleans, Atlanta, or Dallas, it did not matter, Pat always picked up the tab. It got to where I stopped even offering.

The meeting started the following morning at 9 at Pat's office. The offices of the Gloor Law Group were at 225 West Wacker. I stayed at the Holiday Inn right across the bridge near the Merchandise Mart. The walk over that morning was exhilarating. The day was cool and crisp and the excitement of the hustle and bustle of people going to work in downtown Chicago is something I had never experienced. I met the Zurich adjuster, Eric Paulsen, in person for the first time. He was a great guy to work with. Very smart and practical. CNA, another large insurance company similar to Zurich, insured US Blending. Its adjuster was a guy named Kevin Horwitz, another really good guy with whom I became friends. The lawyers and insurance adjuster for Southern Dry Mix were also there.

The meeting was in a conference room overlooking the Chicago River about 25 floors high, directly across the river from the Merchandise Mart building. It, like so many buildings in Chicago, is architecturally stunning. It was built in the 1930s and is a grayish-looking art deco building 25 stories high with row after row of windows. When it was built, it was the largest building in the world with four million square feet. So, here I am with this incredible view out of the window trying to concentrate on the meeting at hand.

The Southern Dry Mix lawyers beat everyone to the punch and suggested US Blending pay 50% and Southern Dry Mix and Complete Body 25% each. Now, at this time, the facts of the case had not been fleshed out. The case was brand new and the purpose of the meeting was to see if a quick resolution could be reached without the insurance companies spending a fortune on legal fees. Of course, a quick resolution is the last thing a defense lawyer wants. Tough to bill hours when the case has been resolved. It quickly became apparent there was no reason to worry about a quick resolution.

Pat countered with a suggested 70-20-10 split with Southern Dry Mix funding 70%, US Blending 20% and Complete Body 10% of a settlement pot. I knew this suggested split was coming and had already agreed to it once I discussed it with Zurich's adjuster. Southern Dry Mix's lawyers and insurance adjuster went ballistic, faces turned red, and voices were raised. It became apparent to them that US Blending and Complete Body had joined forces against them.

With no agreement on an early resolution, the litigation began. The *Complete Body* case spanned three years. It was intellectually challenging. There was the class action/complex litigation part of the case. There were incredible personalities involved on both sides. The travel, although not to exotic places like India, was great. We took depositions in New York City, Dallas, New Orleans, and Chicago, not to mention Scottsboro, Alabama, Crowley, Louisiana, and Chipley, Florida. This case was so big, we had three pre-mediation meetings in Atlanta to prepare for the mediation. There was about $20 million in total insurance coverage available among the defendants to settle the cases. The plaintiffs' lawyers wanted every bit of it.

CHAPTER THIRTY
THE COMPLETE BODY CASE: OFF TO NEW ORLEANS

The actual mediation was a three-day event held at the Ritz-Carlton in New Orleans. The Ritz-Carlton in New Orleans is an amazing hotel. To enter the hotel, you pull into the garage from Canal Street, the western border of the French Quarter. After the valet takes your car, you enter the hotel a floor below the lobby. Elevators run from the lobby to the bottom floor. When the elevator doors open at the bottom floor, the smell of fresh flowers is so strong it almost knocks you down. Upon arrival in the lobby, the smell is even stronger. To the left of the elevator is a 5-foot high bouquet of fresh flowers sitting atop a table generating the aroma. If you are ever in New Orleans, go to the Ritz-Carlton lobby just to experience this smell.

The actual mediation took place in the bottom level where the conference rooms are located. The Boston Celtics were in town to play the then-named New Orleans Hornets. The Celtics were staying at the Ritz. One morning while I was hanging out in the hallway outside the conference rooms during a break in the mediation, I saw Kevin Garnet, Rajon Rondo, and Paul Pierce. The Celtics breakfast was served across the hall from the mediation rooms. The best part of the mediation was it started the Monday after the Saints won the Super Bowl. The city was electric. We mediated the case for a solid three days beginning at 9 o'clock each morning and ending at 5 o'clock in the afternoon. The mediator was a guy named Rod Max. He looked and sounded like Casey Kasem. Rod had made a fortune as a mediator. His mantra was always, "Stick to the process. Believe in the process." The time spent mediating the case was excruciatingly long and boring. Out of the $20 million in insurance coverage, my client only had $2 million. We knew we were going to offer the total amount. The only tricky part was making sure all of the cases were resolved within our coverage limits.

Southern Dry Mix had by far the most insurance coverage, which placed the bull's eye on its back. During the mediation process, all sides knew how much insurance coverage each party had. Because Southern Dry Mix did not offer its full policy limits, the cases did not settle during the mediation.

The evening after the first day of mediation was the Saints' victory parade. The parade went up Canal Street right in front of the Ritz. Don, Pat, Kevin Horwitz, and I had

CHAPTER THIRTY-ONE
THE GURLEY TRIAL

All of the Georgia *Complete Body* cases were pending in DeKalb County, the county seat of which is Decatur, Georgia. Decatur is just northeast of Atlanta. Emory University is in Decatur. Mr. Gurley was the Plaintiff in the case we tried. Mr. Gurley was handpicked by Mark and Joey. This case was basically a test case to see how much a jury would award in one of these cases and what percentage of fault a jury would attach to each of the three Defendants. By the time the *Gurley* case went to trial, each of the three insurance carriers for the three Defendants only had a limited amount of money left to cover the 40 remaining Georgia Plaintiffs. So basically, whatever amount the jury awarded to Mr. Gurley, the remaining Georgia Plaintiffs would split the remaining insurance proceeds. By this time, Complete Body was basically wiped out and had no assets. US Blending was teetering on the brink of bankruptcy. Only Southern Dry Mix was a solvent company. So, it had all the incentive in the world to get these cases settled within the insurance policy limits.

Mr. Gurley was in horrible condition. He was old, frail, and sick. He had several health conditions that were unrelated to his consumption of the tainted Complete Body Formula. By the time the trial began, all of his hair had grown back, as well as his fingernails. Mr. Gurley had congestive heart and renal failure. His lawyers found an "expert witness" from Boston to testify Mr. Gurley's condition was worsened by the excess selenium from Complete Body Formula.

No matter what the case, no matter what testimony a lawyer needs, a lawyer can almost always find an "expert witness" to give the testimony he or she needs. The Defendants countered with highly qualified physicians from Atlanta - a cardiologist and nephrologist. They testified selenium poisoning did not affect Mr. Gurley's congestive heart and renal failure.

One of the perks of this trial was getting to stay in Buckhead. Buckhead is just north of midtown Atlanta. Buckhead exudes wealth. It is a paradise for the younger, moneyed crowd. Trial lasted two weeks. Each day I made the 25-minute drive from Buckhead to Decatur. Atlanta traffic is horrendous. Fortunately, my morning drive was going away from downtown and my afternoon return trip was coming back toward downtown. So each way, I was going the opposite direction of traffic.

The DeKalb County Courthouse was nothing architecturally special. Actually, it was an ugly building, probably built in the 70's. Most importantly though, it was easily accessible. The parking garage was adjacent to the courthouse. I could access the courthouse by a rear entrance only steps from the exit of the parking deck. I can't overstate the importance of accessibility. Trying a case for two weeks is physically and mentally exhausting. I have been to trials before where just getting into the courthouse was a struggle. Most lawyers don't worry or even think about accessibility to the courthouse. Accessibility is just one of those extra things I always have to deal with that most lawyers take for granted.

When trying cases, I also have the added concern of moving around in front of the jury. I try to sit at the end of counsel table so I have an unimpeded path to the podium. The area in most courtrooms where the lawyers are seated, examine witnesses, and make arguments to the jury is relatively small. This works great for me because there is very little walking to do while trying a case. But, with cords on the ground for video equipment and boxes of trial exhibits sitting on the floor, there are all kinds of potential tripping hazards. Each day before trial starts, I plan my route from counsel table to the podium to make sure I have a clear path.

Then there's the shoes' issue. When I'm not in trial, I don't care that the toe of my left shoe is completely worn out with a hole. When in that condition, my shoes are broken in just right. I can't wear worn out shoes to trial. However, brand new dress shoes are a tripping hazard. I hate the first few days of wearing new dress shoes. They are stiff and incredibly difficult to walk in – completely unforgiving. One stub of the toe and look out ground. So, I will buy new shoes about 2 weeks before the trial. That gives me time to break them in but not enough time to wear a hole in the left toe.

I have yet to trip and fall in front of a jury. When I walk to the podium, I focus on each step and ensure that my steps are high enough to where I do not trip. When I am walking toward the jury, I typically look down at the floor as if I am pondering important questions before I reach the podium. Once I reach the podium, I open my binder with examination questions and then begin to engage the jury while questioning the witness. Making my way to the podium is actually a calming exercise. I know all eyes are on me. The jury must be thinking, *what the hell is wrong with that guy?* Maybe even silently playing "guess the condition?" For some reason, whatever nerves I have when I get up to make my way to the action are gone before the first words come out of my mouth.

Trying a jury trial is all about preparation. Once you arrive the first day for jury selection, the hard part is over. Trial is where the fun begins. I arrived in Buckhead the Thursday before the Monday trial to work with my local counsel. Steve Schatz and Steve DeFrank of the Swift Currie firm in Atlanta were local counsel. The great part of trying a case as the out of state lawyer with local counsel is local counsel completes much of the tedious (but incredibly important) work of preparing and numbering exhibits, preparing motions *in limine* to attempt to exclude evidence at trial, and having blowups and trial aides prepared and brought to the courthouse.

Schatz was the managing partner at Swift Currie. He was incredibly sharp and a great guy. The main reason I was lead counsel trying the case instead of Schatz was because I had been living the case for three years and had a greater factual knowledge of it. Schatz was fully capable of handling the case without me. He did *voir dire*. I believe it is always important to have the local lawyer be the first to speak to the local jury. This may be less important in a large metropolitan area like Atlanta, but still, the jury should see a local lawyer represents the defendant.

We tried the case in front of the Honorable Alvin Wong. Judge Wong was one of the best trial judges I had ever tried a case in front of. He allowed the lawyers to try the case but kept the trial moving by excluding extraneous bullshit. He was fair to both sides. Judge Wong even ordered us to try the case on a Saturday to ensure the case would be over within the two-week jury term.

So, Schatz, DeFrank and I made up the Complete Body trial team. US Blending was represented by Jori Young (from Pat Gloor's firm in Chicago), along with local counsel. Jori and I had become really good friends during the litigation process. Pat and Don brought her into the case to handle several of the depositions. After Don suffered a minor stroke, Jori was tabbed as the lawyer to try the case for US Blending. Jori is an exceptionally good trial lawyer. After having a couple of kids, Jori hung up being a lawyer in private practice and took a job with one of the world's largest insurance companies, supervising mass tort claims. Just like with Don and Pat, Jori and I are still good friends.

The case tried for almost two weeks. I had become good friends with both Joey and Mark, Mr. Gurley's lawyers. We would try the case all day, very contentious at times, and then have a drink together during the weekend of the trial. There is a misconception that all plaintiff and defense lawyers in a case don't like each other. Often, that's true, but more often than not, lawyers on opposing sides get along fairly well. I have always thought it was to my client's advantage for the lawyers suing my client to like me. No reason to give a good plaintiff lawyer an extra reason to want to pop my client.

The case tried well for Complete Body. Joey came out of the gate attacking Complete Body hard. Actually, he spent the first three days attacking Complete Body for not testing some of the bottles to ensure the correct amount of vitamins and minerals were in it before distributing it. We went at each other pretty good for the first three days. Joey then turned his attention to the other defendants. The facts against these two companies were bad. Witnesses testified how Southern Dry Mix screwed up the formula for the vitamin and mineral dry mix that caused the excess selenium in the final product. Worse, witnesses testified how Southern Dry Mix attempted to cover up its mistake. Testimony came out about how US Blending employees got sick after sampling batches of the Complete Body Formula but covered it up. It turned out that US Blending strained the product through pantyhose to remove black specks from Complete Body Formula before it was bottled and sent to Larry Brown for distribution. The black specks were just part of the dry mix that were non-soluble in the liquid. They had nothing to do with the excess selenium. The testimony just showed US Blending's shoddy operation.

The jury came back with a verdict of over 2 million dollars. I can't recall the exact amount. The jury apportioned fault 70% Southern Dry Mix, 20% US Blending and 10% against Complete Body. I was disappointed. While only 10% liability was a decent result and the client was happy, I thought I tried a good enough case to win. As mentioned before, it really doesn't matter how good of a case you try when you have bad facts. Also, when your client is sued along with some bad actors, it is hard to completely separate your client from what happened and come out completely unscathed. In the *Complete Body* case, the screw up was in the manufacturing of the product, but my client distributed it without testing it. In retrospect, winning outright was never very likely. 10% fault was not so bad.

Interestingly, the jury's apportionment of fault was the exact percentage mentioned earlier that Pat and I had agreed to present to the Defendants and their insurance carriers back in Chicago when the cases first began. I'm glad the case did not settle at the inception because working on the *Complete Body* case was one of the best experiences of my life.

We concluded the *Complete Body* case in February 2013. About midway through the litigation, Nick Alberts, a claims specialist for Zurich, took over for Eric Paulsen, the original claims specialist. Insurance carriers shift claim's adjusters on files fairly frequently. However, this can cause heartburn for the lawyer. *Complete Body* was very complex, lengthy, and hotly contested. I became very good friends with Eric Paulsen. We spoke on a daily basis about the case, traveled together and resolved all the cases other than the Georgia cases. Now I had to begin working with someone completely new. I had no idea how the case would proceed or whether working on it would be as enjoyable. Most claims adjusters are fairly easy to work with, but sometimes you run into a real ass.

My initial concerns about reporting to a new adjuster dissipated quickly. Nick and I developed a very good relationship. Following the verdict in the *Gurley* trial, Complete Body settled the remaining Georgia cases, and the odyssey came to an end. Nick sent me a great email closing out the case in which he said: *"I very much enjoyed working with you, and you really set the bar on all fronts for what it means to be a great defense attorney. For whatever it may be worth, I gave you perfect marks in my closing evaluation. I will continue to sing your praises to my co-workers, and if I have another chance, I will hire you again in a second. If all of the attorneys with whom we work were half as good as you, my colleagues and I would be thrilled. Thanks again and take care, Rod. Nick."*

CHAPTER THIRTY-THREE
SCENES FROM AN ITALIAN RESTAURANT

Tripping and falling is something that I've had to deal with. Falling is no fun, especially in front of a bunch of people. Falling is just part of the deal. But what sucks is when I fall and it's not my fault. If I go down just because I failed to pick my foot off the ground and tripped, tough shit for me. But when something beyond my control causes me to fall, it kind of pisses me off. In other words, I don't need any help falling.

As an example, my wife, kids, and I were leaving a local Italian restaurant after dinner one night. Corbit, who was a senior in high school at the time, stayed behind with me. As we were walking out, I put my cane down under a table as the tables were real close together. As soon as I put pressure on the cane, it slipped out from me. There was some liquid on the floor that was incredibly slick. I had all of my weight on the cane when it slipped out. I went down hard and fast. This was actually one of my hardest falls. I was expecting my cane to grip the floor as normal so was not expecting it to shoot out from under me. I was on the floor face down instantly. I went down so fast I hit my face above my left eye and bent my glasses, which went shooting across the floor. I went down so fast I did not have time to think about protecting myself.

So I'm down. The worst part of this ordeal is the collective sound the other diners make as I crashed to the ground. It sounds somewhat like a loud: *"ohhhhh!"* followed by: *"Nooooo!"* My first thought as I am face down on the floor is: *"Did my glasses break?"* No, just bent. Am I bleeding where I hit the floor above my eye? Don't think so. The embarrassment of falling face first in front of a crowded restaurant is pervasive in all my thoughts. The anger, no just pissed - anger is too strong a word - from falling because of a slick floor enters my brain. I just wanted to get up and get out of there.

Someone rushes over to help me. My daughter finds my glasses about ten feet away from where my face planted on the concrete floor. Thank goodness there is a bench close to where I fell so I could push myself up on my own. Getting up by myself takes some of the sting out of the humiliation. The owner comes over to ask if I am okay, probably worried about a slip and fall lawsuit. I respond that I'm fine and make no mention of the slick floor and walk out the door with all the dignity I can muster, which was not much. My daughter starts to cry when we drive off. I thought she was crying because of the embarrassment she felt by being there when her father fell. It can't be easy for children of a handi who falls. No one wants to see their Dad fall down in front of a bunch of people and hear the "wail" of the crowd. She told me she was crying because it hurts her inside to see me fall and go through what I do. She knows falling is embarrassing to me. She knows my pride takes a hit. I have a wonderful daughter.

By the time I arrived back home, I was over the falling incident. I like to keep the "falling-public humiliation-embarrassment" down to a minimum, but I know it's going to happen. So it does no one any good for me to stew over a fall. I've learned to move on to the next thing quickly. Plus, before my spectacular exit, we had some great pizza.

CHAPTER THIRTY-FOUR
DON'T GO CHASING WATERSLIDES

Going through life the way I do with my physical limitations has taught me to swallow my pride and check my ego at the door. I have learned an incredible amount of humility. I know that if I want to participate in the non-handi world, being thin-skinned, embarrassed, or worried about what others think is not an option. There is nothing cool about the way I walk. I just look weird. But, if I worried about what I look like when I walk or engage in physical activities, I would never leave my house. I am incredibly active for someone who is a quadriplegic.

I like waterslides. Maybe since I'm 52 years old, irrespective of my condition, I should give up waterslides. Not yet. During one of our annual 4th of July trip to the Great Smoky Mountains, we stayed at a place called Wilderness Lodge in Sevierville, Tennessee. This place has great waterslides. I had seen on TV, but never had ridden, a waterslide where you step into a tube, stand on a floor, count down to zero, the floor falls away and you plunge straight down. Wilderness Lodge has just this waterslide. I was not going to be denied. So I left my pride at the table where my family was sitting and walked over to the flights of stairs I had to climb to get to the waterslide.

Once I arrived at the bottom of the stairs, I gave my cane to my sister Lisa, who walked over to the end of the waterslide where the tube spits you out and you eventually come to a stop. The end of the slide consists of about 50 yards of flat fiberglass with approximately 3-foot tall sides. My other sister Valerie is behind me making this trudge up the stairs. The stairs are used to access two waterslides. One slide is where you sit on a rubber raft and go down the slide at a pretty good rate of speed and then when you get to the bottom your speed takes you straight up a big pink wall that looks like a giant tongue. It is similar to a half pipe for a skateboard but much taller and wider. I had ridden this slide earlier. While a lot of fun, I saw no comparison between that waterslide and the tube with the trapdoor floor.

Only a few people were in the line for the trapdoor floor waterslide. So while climbing up the stairs, we did not have to wait behind the people waiting to ride the other waterslide. I have to use a rail to climb stairs. So up I go, excusing myself as people eventually understood I had a disability requiring me to hold the rail as I climbed the stairs. I'm doing this without a cane in my hand so there is no signal to people that I have physical limitation other than the obvious. By the time I reached the top, five flights later, any sense of ego, pride, cool, etc. was gone.

There is nothing cool about a 52-year-old guy, wearing a bathing suit and pool shoes climbing five flights of stairs and struggling with each step as the people who I go by stare wondering what's wrong with me. I have a feeling of complete nakedness. I feel I have nothing left inside me that is private. I have nothing to hide. I'm just a disabled dude out there for the world to see who is not going to miss out on life because of how I look doing things that require some physical effort. This feeling is not limited to waterslides, but in everything I do. You can't hide when you walk like I do. I am on display for the world to see with every ugly step I take. But, I'm just not going to miss out on life no matter how weird I look.

So I'm at the top of the platform. No cane. I have to "Spiderman" it – clinging to the outside rail to get to the opening of the tube. I finally arrive. There was this teenage girl who is running the show. She watches me struggling to get to the door of the tube. I look over at her. She has this look on her face that says, "*You've got to be freaking kidding me!*" I had my pool shoes on. She tells me they have to go. So my sister reaches down to help me take them off. I have to step over a ledge which I do by reaching down with my hand right above the back of my right knee and help lift my leg over. I pull my left leg behind me, scraping the top of my left foot over the ledge as I get in the tube. It quickly reminded me of how I hate bathtub showers that have sliding glass doors. I always scrape the skin on my left shin getting into a bathtub shower as I never pull my left leg up high enough to get in before it scrapes on the metal where the door slides. I have a walk-in shower at home.

I'm in the tube. I'm standing with my heels on the back of this trapdoor. My arms are crossed over my chest. My head is pressed to the back of the tube. I'm basically vertical with a slight lean to the back. The girl, who I'm sure has never seen a circus like this, starts the countdown, three (then I start thinking - Is this really a good idea?), two (too late now anyway), one (Shit!). The trapdoor falls away and I fall straight down the tube. The speed is so fast that it overcomes gravity and the tube goes uphill after reaching the bottom and loops around before spitting me out onto the flat fiberglass slowdown and exit area.

So I come to a stop. I struggle to my knees, and with the help of my sisters, make it off the slide. I now have my cane and start walking to the stairs where I can sit and put my pool shoes back on. Several people saw me struggling to get off the slide and watched me walk barefoot with my cane to the stairs. Many people asked me how it was. I responded that it was awesome, very fast, a lot of fun. The truth is it was incredible. The rush was like nothing I had ever experienced before. As I was walking back to join the rest of my family, I was thinking, if I would not have swallowed my pride to climb those stairs and decided to stay where it was comfortable and not say, "*Screw it, I'm doing this,*" I would have never experienced the thrill of plunging through a tube of water.

This is just a vignette of how I've lived my life. I want the thrill of the waterslide. I want to experience as much as a non-disabled person does. I have not allowed this whole being an ambulatory quadriplegic thing stop me. I do have to swallow my pride and ego by putting myself out there and not hiding when I want to accomplish things that are difficult for a handi. But once I do it, the pride and ego I lose in looking weird in front of other people return exponentially once I accomplish what I set out to do.

What I struggle with and go through every day is really not much different than anyone else. We all have struggles. We all have conditions that affect how we live and what we accomplish. You have to do whatever it takes to get to the point where you are standing on the trapdoor. You cannot allow how you think others will perceive you to affect your journey. You cannot reach your goals, whether they be work, financial, raising a family, or whatever it is if you are constantly worrying about what others are thinking of you. It takes focus on yourself and your goals.

I know I look weird when I walk. I will not look at myself on video. I will not watch myself when I walk when I see my reflection. I just don't like to see it. But I know other people see me every day and wonder what is wrong with me. And that's okay. I am accustomed to the stares, the inquiries, the offers to help. A week never goes by when I'm walking across the street and someone asks me if I need help. Knowing what I have accomplished given the hand I was dealt gives me a sense of pride far more than the hit to my ego when someone asks if I need help crossing the street. I'm so unique with my disability and limitations that I'm not sure at this point in life I would change anything if I could. I'm defined by my disability, but in a good way. I'm a guy who did not quit. I'm a guy who refused to let a disability change the way I live my life.

If you take any message away from reading this book, I hope it is – don't quit, ever! I could have quit from day one of being paralyzed. I could have felt sorry for myself because so much was taken from me and just said, "*I'm done.*" I could have quit when it sunk in for the first time that although I could walk, I'd walk like a freak for the rest of my life. I could have quit the first time I fell and broke my finger. But then, I would not have had the joy of breaking my finger two more times. I could have quit after the embarrassment of being rejected by a girl because of my disability. You never know what is going to be around the corner. Everything in my life has not worked out great. But if you quit before you get to the corner, you'll never find out what you might accomplish. Not quitting requires a level of toughness. If nothing else, I've become tough through this ordeal. I've gotten to a place where I believe I can handle anything that comes my way. And that feels pretty good.

CHAPTER THIRTY-FIVE
PUTTING IT ALL TOGETHER

I've gotten to the point where I can mentally back away from situations and look at life more philosophically. This is what I believe: Life is not fair. Life will disappoint you. Life is tough. But life is wonderful. I've already lived one of the greatest lives of anyone. Sure, I'm a quadriplegic ... but since becoming one, I've graduated valedictorian from high school, graduated Phi Beta Kappa from Davidson College, obtained my JD/MBA from University of North Carolina Chapel Hill, and have a great career that has given me professional satisfaction and literally taken me half-way around the world. I actually try cases. Think about it, a guy walking all weird trying cases in front of a jury. How awesome. I have a great family, both immediate and extended, have great friends, and have been able to travel throughout the United States and the world. I've been to the Taj Mahal for Christ's sake. None of this would have happened had I quit.

I live with passion. I live with excitement. I enjoy doing small things in life as much or more than the big things. Having a great workout, taking a great nap, having a great sandwich, being with my kids, spending a weekend with my college buds, talking on the phone with my best friend from high school, enjoying other people's successes, having great friends with meaningful relationships. It goes on ....

Find enjoyment in the small things in life. Live with excitement and passion over the small things. We all have one life; why not make it the best? Why not make it so damn enjoyable you can barely contain yourself? I think psychiatrists call it being "self-actualized" - being happy with yourself. I've told my kids the way they need to go through life is to look at themselves as a train engine on the track. The track is their life. They set their goals as the engine to go as fast, as slow, or as far as they want on the track. But their focus needs to be the track in front of them -their life. Other people can join their life and hook onto their engine like boxcars, but they are in control of their own decisions and their own happiness and can pull others along with them. I've told them they do not need to be the boxcars or the cabooses. They need to be the engines. They need to control their own lives. Of course, life doesn't follow smoothly down a track. A train comes to a switch yard where it may end up on one of several tracks. Just like life. Oftentimes, you don't get to choose your track. But you've got to make the best of the track you're on. You just don't want to derail.

Living with passion and excitement does not mean being in constant motion or always doing something. Chilling can be done with passion. I wake up each morning at 4:30 and go work out. One of my favorite things to do is come home after my workout, eat a bowl of cereal and watch 20 minutes of Squawk Box (the best show on TV) on CNBC to catch up on the business news. I love this time of just relaxing before getting the work day going. I also flip over to the Weather Channel to see how Stephanie Abrams is looking (admittedly creeping a bit).

I'm not sure why I've developed this passion for life after going through a devastating life changing event. Maybe it's that I feel like I've been given a second chance in life. I've really lived two lives: the athlete kid/teenager whose life could not have been any better and the adult who has gone through life with a major disability. I rarely, if ever, have a depressed day wallowing in self-pity. I know you may find that hard to believe, but my mind just does not allow me to be depressed. I have too many things to be thankful for. Maybe I know how much worse things could have been. Struggling to walk is much better than being wheelchair bound. Breathing on my own is much better than being on a ventilator. Being alive is much better than being dead. Hell, I've got it all!

Maybe being physically disabled takes pressure off of trying to impress people, trying to be something you're not. People do not expect much from the physically disabled. When I'm traveling through airports making small talk with the person I'm sitting beside on a plane and tell them what I do, they generally seem astonished that someone who walks like I do is a lawyer who regularly travels and tries cases. When I work out, I have so many people tell me that I'm such an inspiration to them. People are surprised to see someone with a major disability be so active. So, I have little to live up to. That gives me a sense of freedom to not impress others, which allows me to focus on what I want to do. When I am doing what I enjoy and being successful at it, I become incredibly passionate and excited.

I'm not sure where and when this odyssey will end. If I get hit by a truck on the way home tonight, I can say that it's been one hell of a ride. I figure I have about ten more years of being a lawyer and physically able to try cases. I hope to try at least a couple more cases before it is all over. I want to travel to some places I've never been before my disability progresses to where I am not able to enjoy traveling. But most importantly, I want to continue living as if I'm one of the luckiest guys on the face of the Earth that was given a gift of 15 years of an incredible childhood and early teen years and an even greater gift of living the rest of my life with a physical disability that could have been so much worse.

We all have limitations and disabilities. Don't let them define you in a bad way. Use them to your advantage. They make you unique. Be passionate. Live with an excitable purpose. The clock is ticking on this one life we have. It's not about anyone else. It's about you.

CHAPTER THIRTY-SIX
PARTING SHOTS: MY TWO CENTS

Very few, if any, people have a smooth upward trajectory on how their life goes. Using a basic chart with "time" on the x-axis and "success," "happiness," "achievements" or whatever word you want to use for the y-axis, most likely everyone's chart will have its ups and downs. If the general trajectory is up toward the right, that is great. However, many people live lives that have no upward trajectory. Life can be a constant ass-whip. Based on my experiences in the 52 years I have been on this earth, these are my thoughts on how to achieve the most fulfilling, rewarding, and happy life as possible (a general upward trajectory):

- Understand that this is your one life. When it's over, it's over. On a tombstone there is typically a date of birth and a date of death with a dash in between. The dash is your life. Figure out what it takes for you to live your best life. Is it a successful job? Is it making a bunch of money? Is it helping others? Is it having fun? Is it a combination of multiple things? Figure it out, find your groove and get moving. Even if you don't know exactly what you want to do, do something. Make mistakes. But live.

- Live with passion and inspiration. It really comes down to having a positive outlook. Even when I fall, I keep getting up. A positive outlook means not feeling sorry for yourself. Every day is not going to be great. Every experience you go through is not going to be great. But every experience is an experience, and that's what makes life. Find pleasure in the small things in life. Nothing to me is ordinary. I still marvel at life and my surroundings on a daily basis. I marveled at the Taj Mahal. I marvel when I watch different types of birds flocking to my birdfeeder in the backyard. When things don't go your way, plan on how to work through it. My plan when I broke my neck was to pretend that my physical limitations did not exist. After the three-month hiatus in the hospital and rehab center, I went right back to living my life. I got a great education. I've had a great career. I have a great family. This would not have happened had I gone through life with a chip on my shoulder or pissed off at the world for having such a shitty hand dealt to me. We all have bad hands dealt to us.

- There is no substitute for hard work. I've worked hard all my life. I worked in the tobacco fields in the summertime in North Carolina. Never have I worked a job harder than that. I worked hard on my studies, graduating valedictorian of my high school and Phi Beta Kappa from college. During the 25 years I've been a lawyer, I've worked extremely hard on my cases. I'm at the gym by 5:00 o'clock every morning to exercise. There is nothing better than coming home after a day of hard work and feeling good about yourself for really busting your ass. The luckiest people in the world are the ones who work the hardest.

- Slow down. Take time to reflect on your life. The next thing is always the most important. However, it is also important to take an inventory of your life. Before moving forward, it is good to understand what you have done, what has worked, what has not worked, and what makes you happy. When I stop to reflect on my life, I think how fortunate I have been. I was a kid who grew up in small, country towns. I was never exposed to anything that would be characterized as cultural. I had a great childhood playing sports. I had a horrible accident. My accident did not derail me. I'm sitting here at 52 years-old. I struggle physically every day. It is part of what I am. I have had incredible life accomplishments that, regardless of what happens in the future, can never be taken away.

- Don't take yourself too seriously. You have to be able to laugh at yourself. So many people get offended over the smallest things. Maybe because of my physical condition, I have developed extremely thick skin. Everyone should have thick skin. I laugh so hard when my son Cullen and I are talking and I make a statement something to the effect that, *"I'm going to run to the store."* Cullen will look at me and say, *"You can't run anywhere because"* and then he makes the quotation symbol in the air and whispers *"you're handicapped."* It is hilarious.

- Depression-proof your life. I do not understand depression. That does not mean it doesn't exist. I've seen depression firsthand in my family. I have just never felt that things are so bad that I have undergone a sustained "blue" period. Part of depression-proofing your life is to try to put into practice the bullet points listed above. Based upon what I have seen, depression and loneliness go hand-in-hand. I've seen people that have become down, sad, and hopeless and when they don't have a good support system, they continue to spiral downward.

- One of the most important keys to happiness is to have great relationships. I have been fortunate in that I have so many great relationships: friends, family, schoolmates and co-workers. You need to have a network of people with whom you can share your goals and dreams and, most importantly, share your disappointments, fears and mistakes. In order to develop great relationships, you cannot be a net taker in a relationship. Don't be an emotional drain. In order to develop great relationships, you have to truly give a shit about the other person. And you can't fake it. Once other people realize that you truly care about them and their well-being and want good things to happen to them, your desire for their success will result in great relationships. Life is so much better when successes and disappointments are shared with people who truly give a shit about you and who you truly give a shit about.

- Finally, and this last one is a hard one - work on being a good person. Make an effort to be good. Make an effort to be supportive. Make an effort to be moral. Make an effort to be truthful. Make an effort to be reliable. This, of course, will constantly be a work in progress, and you may never reach your goals of being that good person. I know I haven't, but I try. We all have dark sides. But it's the mindset you have and the effort to step back from a situation and look at your actions to realize if you are going down a good path or not.

Take these steps now. Don't wait until the weekend is over and say I'll start on Monday. These steps can either turn your life around or keep you going in the right direction. Remember, you only have one life. Make it great, and make it great now. To use a sports saying: "Leave it all out on the field." I'll leave you with my favorite quote from A.A. Milne:

"What day is it?"
"It's today," squeaked Piglet.
"My favorite day," said Pooh.

ACKNOWLEDGEMENTS

Thank you to the following individuals for their insights, constructive criticisms, and assistance in making this project a reality:

Andrew Countyman, Don Ivansek, Pat Gloor, David Lilley, Vince Gaddy, Tom Oldweiler, Crawford Binion, Dhiren Kapadia, Michael Upchurch, Jennifer Miles and Barbara Rembert.

Made in the USA
Lexington, KY
23 November 2019